This Explicit Grace

Yes, It's Sufficient

Volume Three

**The
SOME THINGS MADE PLAIN
Series**

Theresa Kirk

This Explicit Grace

Volume 3 of Some Things Made Plain
By Theresa Kirk

KNOWLEDGE POWER BOOKS
25379 Wayne Mills Place, Suite 131, Valencia, CA 91355
www.knowledgepowerbooks.com

Edited by:
Gena Clayton & Penny Scott

Jacket Design and Photography:
Juan Roberts of Creative Lunacy
CreativeLunacy1.blogspot.com

Interior Design - **John Sibley - Rock Solid Productions**
www.rocksolidgraphicarts.com

Library of Congress Control Number: 2010938173
ISBN 978-0-9854107-7-3

A Gift To

From

This Explicit Grace

Yes, It's Sufficient

CONTENTS

DEDICATION

To my Beautiful Mother, Ellinor

I dedicate the third volume to you because not only are you my life source, but while I was writing each page of this volume, you saluted me along the way. You encouraged me with your words of wisdom, love, and support. Mom, you are a treasure. I am certain that God is pleased each time He looks in your direction. It didn't matter the hour of the day or night, you were willing lend me a golden nugget to scribe. Thank you, Grannie. I am glad God chose you for me and me for you. You told each of us, Jimmy, Angela, and David that God was real and He alone loved us more than anyone ever would or possibly could. You also told us that His love had a calling attached to our lives that was sure. Well, each time I write I remember those words and therefore continue my writing ministry journey. I Love You today and forever.

Your Daughter, Theresa
~TeeCee

ACKNOWLEDGEMENTS

Every teacher must first be a good student. I celebrate each teacher that I have had the pleasure to sit with and learn. I honor each person that I was given the opportunity to teach. Because in either case, I was learning. Whether you were my Pastors, Dr. Fred and Linda Hodge, or a good friend, there was something I took from each of you along this journey. You helped me to complete what God Himself orchestrated to be a part of my life. I salute each person that told me to press on when at times I wanted to quit. Each encouraging word has allowed me to complete the third volume of this series. I give glory and honor to the wisdom of the Holy Spirit for allowing me to have a deeper understanding of our God's *Explicit Grace* as I was writing. My editor and dear friend, Gena Anderson, I am so blessed God put us together. My publisher Willa Robinson (Mom Willa), God knew what He was doing when He sent you my way. Thank you for ***everything***. Angela Scott, what a gifted scribe you are. I pray blessings in your direction always. Divine Divas, I love you! Chelsea & Jaylon, I am blessed that God trusts me with your lives. I could not imagine my life without either of you. Living Praise Christian Center family, we have greatest church in world. Lastly, the Woven cabinet, I am honored to work along side of each of you amazing women of God.

With many applauds & careful prayers I Thank you all for being a part of my life!

Theresa Kirk

PRAISE

When reading this book you get the revelation of how Grace is the favor of God. It's the ability to live this life uncompromised by the things that the enemy will throw at you on a daily basis. It's the knowledge to understand the power and authority of the Almighty God that we serve. And how if we bend but don't break under the pressure of Satan, that God will keep pouring into us and allowing us to grow in the knowledge and the revelation of the spirit realm and to step into our full calling of a victorious spirit.

Theresa, thank you for being obedient to allow God to use you to bless the people of God. You are a precious jewel.

Pastors Wilbur & Geri Ayers
Living Praise Christian Center, Chatsworth, California

EPISODE ONE

WHO IS THIS GOD?

Psalms 148:13 (NKJV)

Let them praise the name of the Lord,
For His name alone is exalted;
His glory is above the earth and heaven.

WERE YOU THERE?

Job 38 (MSG)

And now, finally, GOD answered Job from the eye of a violent storm. He said:

"Why do you confuse the issue?
Why do you talk without knowing what you're talking about?
Pull yourself together, Job!
Up on your feet! Stand tall!
I have some questions for you,
and I want some straight answers.
Where were you when I created the earth?
Tell me, since you know so much!
Who decided on its size? Certainly you'll know that!
Who came up with the blueprints and measurements?
How was its foundation poured,
and who set the cornerstone,
While the morning stars sang in chorus
and all the angels shouted praise?
And who took charge of the ocean
when it gushed forth like a baby from the womb?
That was me! I wrapped it in soft clouds,
and tucked it in safely at night.
Then I made a playpen for it,
a strong playpen so it couldn't run loose,
And said, 'Stay here, this is your place.
Your wild tantrums are confined to this place.'

"And have you ever ordered Morning, 'Get up!'
told Dawn, 'Get to work!'
So you could seize Earth like a blanket
and shake out the wicked like cockroaches?

This Explicit Grace

As the sun brings everything to light,
brings out all the colors and shapes,
The cover of darkness is snatched from the wicked—
they're caught in the very act!
"Have you ever gotten to the true bottom of things,
explored the labyrinthine caves of deep ocean?
Do you know the first thing about death?
Do you have one clue regarding death's dark mysteries?
And do you have any idea how large this earth is?
Speak up if you have even the beginning of an answer.

"Do you know where Light comes from
and where Darkness lives
So you can take them by the hand
and lead them home when they get lost?
Why, of *course* you know that.
You've known them all your life,
grown up in the same neighborhood with them!

"Have you ever traveled to where snow is made,
seen the vault where hail is stockpiled,
The arsenals of hail and snow that I keep in readiness
for times of trouble and battle and war?
Can you find your way to where lightning is launched,
or to the place from which the wind blows?
Who do you suppose carves canyons
for the downpours of rain, and charts
the route of thunderstorms
That bring water to unvisited fields,
deserts no one ever lays eyes on,
Drenching the useless wastelands
so they're carpeted with wildflowers and grass?
And who do you think is the father of rain and dew,
the mother of ice and frost?

Episode One ~ Who Is This God?

You don't for a minute imagine
these marvels of weather just happen, do you?

"Can you catch the eye of the beautiful Pleiades sisters,
or distract Orion from his hunt?
Can you get Venus to look your way,
or get the Great Bear and her cubs to come out and play?
Do you know the first thing about the sky's constellations
and how they affect things on Earth?
"Can you get the attention of the clouds,
and commission a shower of rain?
Can you take charge of the lightning bolts
and have them report to you for orders?
"Who do you think gave weather-wisdom to the ibis,
and storm-savvy to the rooster?
Does anyone know enough to number all the clouds
or tip over the rain barrels of heaven
When the earth is cracked and dry,
the ground baked hard as a brick?

"Can you teach the lioness to stalk her prey
and satisfy the appetite of her cubs
As they crouch in their den,
waiting hungrily in their cave?
And who sets out food for the ravens
when their young cry to God,
fluttering about because they have no food?"

"I AM was there were you?"

MY GLORY

Psalm 3:3 (ESV)

But you, O LORD, are a shield about me, my glory, and the lifter of my head.

Glory~ adoring praise or worshipful thanksgiving:
Give glory to God.

I remember hearing as a young girl my Mee-Maw, and even my Mother say, "When I think of His goodness and all that He's done for me I praise Him even more." Well, as an adult now, I have my reasons to say the same. As I read this scripture, I can say, "He has been my shield even in times when I was unaware. He is my reason to worship as often as I chose, and for the night seasons. That for awhile, lasted longer than the average night. Yes, you guessed it! He was the lifter of my head." This makes me grateful that I was exposed at early age: to understanding the importance of praising God. There are so many reasons to praise: even if in my praise I sometimes cry. He is always right there to wipe away my tears. Then, confirm His Word: when the morning comes, my weeping really did only last for the night. And with this new day, I can choose to cry in it or rejoice. Either way I have a shield. And my head has been lifted up.

Nevertheless Christian:

"I purpose to give the Glory to my shield
who is the lifter of my head."

THE DAYS MAN

Job 9:33 (KJV)

Neither is there any days man betwixt us, that might lay his hands upon us both.

Days Man ~ an umpire; mediator.

Baseball, is where my mind went first when I saw this definition. However, since it is not one of my favorite sports, I did have to do a little homework. My study source was Jaylon. Here's my 1st and only question to my sport savvy son; What is the job of an umpire? Jaylon easily replies, "He is the one who calls all the plays. He or she watches with a keen eye to ensure all rules are followed and the players play fair." Moments later, Jaylon came back with this truth. He said, "Mom, it's like Jesus, when we get to Heaven and stand before God, it will be Jesus who says whether or not we landed properly on base. Or if, we in fact, have struck out." The God we serve is so in love with us, that He makes a serious decision to mediate our very case. Jesus is the true Mediator between God and all humanity. Job understood that if there were no arbitrator, his trials would not be intervened fairly. The reality is that even in the midst of turmoil he was aware that lest his Days Man interceded on his behalf, his opinion was that his suffering would have been in complete vain. Still confused? Well, if that is not enough to satisfy your curious soul, take it a step further. Proceed and turn a few pages until you find yourself in the New Testament, in the book of 1 Corinthians 10:13: **No temptation has overtaken you except such as is common to man; but God *is* faithful, who will not allow you to be tempted beyond what you are able, but with the temptation will also make the way of escape, that you may be able to bear** *it. S*ounds to me like this umpire (**Jesus**) stays on His post; checks all points necessary, verifies with the coach (**Holy Spirit**), confirms with the base watchers (**watchmen**); and maybe even touch base with a few cheerleaders (**angels**). The final score is calculated, and the results are….Heaven take all. The bottom line ….your victory was not a forfeit; and the opponent has thrown in the towel. Your coach ensured you were not a quitter from the start…The creator only chose and created winners for HIS glory team.

"Fear what? Our umpire, Days Man, Mediator, Arbitrator speaks on our behalf."

HOLY THINKING

Leviticus 11:44 (ESV)

For I am the LORD who brought you up out of the land of Egypt to be your God. You shall therefore be holy, for I am holy."

Holy is defined
Dedicated or devoted to the service of God, the church, or religion: Saintly, Godly; pious; devout: a holy life. Having a spiritually pure quality, entitled to worship or adoration.

Psalms 96:9
Worship the LORD in the splendor of holiness; tremble before him, all the earth!

Isaiah 6:3
And one called to another and said: "Holy, holy, holy is the LORD of hosts; the whole earth is full of his glory!"

Hebrews 12:4
Strive for peace with everyone, and for the holiness without which no one will see the Lord.

1 Timothy 2:2
Romans 12:1I appeal to you therefore, brothers, by the mercies of God, to present your bodies as a living sacrifice, holy and acceptable to God, which is your spiritual worship.

Deuteronomy 7:6
"For you are a people holy to the LORD your God. The LORD your God has chosen you to be a people for his treasured possession, out of all the peoples who are on the face of the earth.

If you can train your mind to Holy Thinking, you will please the ONE who requires it...for HE said be Holy for I am Holy...therefore in order to be HOLY you must have Holy Thinking ♥

STRONG TOWER

Psalm 61:3 (NKJV)

Hear my cry, O God; Attend to my prayer.
From the end of the earth, I will cry to You. When my heart is overwhelmed;
Lead me to the ***rock*** *that is higher than I.*
For You have been a ***shelter*** *for me,*
A ***strong tower*** *from the enemy. I will abide in Your tabernacle forever;*
I will trust in the shelter of Your wings.
Selah

Strong; of great force, effectiveness, potency, or cogency; is compelling:

Tower; strength, one relied on for support, or comfort, especially in times of difficulty.

A metaphoric canvas painted, not with oil base paint, or the finest bristled brush. Not at all. In fact, this was David's vivid & colorful expression of the God who he himself chased after for reasons we will continue to find throughout the scripture. We can even look in our own lives. He has allowed this awesome Word to fall into our hands. And then, like David once revealed to us: melt this newfound love and revelation into our hearts and cause a life of transformation. David uses four very intense, yet very descriptive words to create a mental image of the Lord he wants us to know. David expressed that when he is overwhelmed, he looked to his righteous source. He described with these four picturesque, illustrative, and very expressive words, a **shelter**, a **high rock**, a **fortified tower**, and then concludes that as does a mother hen, He shelters us with **outstretched wings.** Think of the gallery which holds a precious piece of mastery genius. The only difference, you are the essence of the completed Masters-Piece. In fact, when the blank canvas was first put into perspective, your life with all its trials and troubles along with a few tears for the overwhelming times, created the colors and its perfected theme. My finished piece, would be in a spray of spring colors; scales of yellow, orange, green, and a hint of soft pallet blues. And, for the overwhelming times, you may see shadows of gray, but nothing darker than these soft hues. For when the times were stony, or unleveled, I chose **His shelter** that sat up on a **High Rock** in a **fortified tower,** which He provided where **His wings** covered me and kept me intact and safe.

"Forever grateful for the Masters-piece that is timeless for all generations."

BRIGHT & MORNING STAR

2 Samuel 23:4 (KJV)

And he shall be as the light of the morning, when the sun riseth, even a morning without clouds; as the tender grass springing out of the earth by clear shining after rain.

Nothing comes to mind at least for me that I can think of more when I unravel this scripture, than the morning after an all night rain. My mind's eye quickly takes me on a visual journey to the memories I have of a very clear, crisp air. And the empowering benefits of this refreshing downpour from heaven. For whatever the reason, children were told rain was God's tears. Well yes, we all believed that for a fleeting moment: until we understood God in nature, along with His eternal season's timetable. Whatever the case, once revealed we see why He would not be crying after the drizzle or downpour. His earth would reap a gracious cleansing. Some areas would experience a plentiful harvest. Was David speaking prophetically when he uttered these words? Consider Revelations 22:16, when Christ looks back to David and declares, "I am the Root and the Offspring of David, the "Bright and Morning Star." Every time we were outside at dusk, my grandmother used to say, "There's the 1st star of the night, make a wish." I would repeat the words she taught me, which at this tender young age I believed was some sort of prayer. "I wish I may, I wish I might, the 1st star I see tonight." I would close my eyes, and make my prayerful wish. Forever, will I hold the dusk times in my heart as a treasured memory with Me-Maw. However, I must confess. I wish I had been told sooner about this "Bright and Morning Star." Maybe, just maybe, I would have turned those wishes to prayers, and not have to keep wishing that same thing dusk after dusk: never seeing it manifest. Had I known to pray to the "Bright and Morning Star," well, you understand. My treasured memories of dusk, I will always hold close to my heart. However, I wonder after all this time. Since Me-Maw was an early riser, was she, in fact, standing in proxy, praying for our future generations? Therefore, saying that she was praying to the "Bright and Morning Star." You know what I mean; you have often heard this repeated, "I know someone was praying for me." Well, I have to believe the prayers that went up, came down to refresh us all in the proper season, according to God's heavenly timetable.

"No more wishes to the Bright & Morning Star, Pray to the Bright & Morning Star."

EXCELLENT IS HE

Psalm 148:13 (KJV)

Let them praise the name of the LORD: for his name alone is excellent, his glory is above the earth and heaven.

Sister Dominique was my 6th grade teacher at Maria Regina Catholic School, and she was not very nice. She rarely smiled at least not in my direction. I can remember my stomach would be upset on the drive to school for the first few months of the new school year. Surely, the question has now come to the forefront of your minds, what does this have to do with the excellence of our Lord? Well, I am glad you asked; halfway through that year I realized why she never smiled in my area of the room. One day I had to take a note home for my parents to sign. The note simply read: "Theresa Antoinette does not fully apply herself in my class." Needless to say, I got a pretty hot chat that night. And then to top it off, the next day I was the first to be called to the chalk board to solve not just one, but two math equations. The chalkboard moment lasted for what seemed to be a million years. However, before I could race my way back to my seat, Sister Dominique exclaimed, "EXCELLENT." Before you start thinking that I am comparing my excellence on that day to the grand and very superior excellence of our Lord, allow me to explain. Excellence is defined as: superior, possessing outstanding quality or great merit; remarkably good, extraordinary. If that single affirmation made me feel like I was on top of the word at 12 years of age. What does this word do to the Lord of Heaven and Earth? When you stop for a moment to remember to say this word from a place of reverence, we acknowledge that we know Him to be EXCELLENT in all His ways. The Word states, in Psalm 150:2 (KJV): Praise him for his mighty acts: praise him according to his excellent greatness. Then it goes on to say it again this way in Psalm 148:13 (KJV): Let them praise the name of the LORD: for his name alone is excellent; his glory is above the earth and heaven. Let me share a wise and true revelation, God is not obligated to stand up to our frivolous words or dialogue. However, when we repeat His written word He stands at our attention. Therefore responding to our request, and or praise because we acknowledged Him for who He is…and Excellent indeed is He…

"Lord you are Excellent in all your ways…I love you forever…."

HE SAID

Matthew 4:4 (KJV)

But he answered and said, It is written, Man shall not live by bread alone, but by every word that proceedeth out of the mouth of God.

John 17:12 (AMP)
While I was with them, I kept and preserved them in Your Name in the knowledge and worship of You. Those You have given Me I guarded and protected, and not one of them has perished or is lost except the son of perdition Judas Iscariot--the one who is now doomed to destruction, destined to be lost], that the Scripture might be fulfilled.

Genesis 1:14 (KJV)
God said, Let there be lights in the firmament of the heaven to divide the day from the night; and let them be for signs, and for seasons, and for days, and years:

Hebrews 13:5 (KJV)
Let your conversation be without covetousness; and be content with such things as ye have: for he hath said, I will never leave thee, nor forsake thee.

Genesis 1:3 (KJV)
God said, Let there be light: and there was light.

Exodus 3:14 (KJV)
God said unto Moses, I AM THAT I AM: and he said, Thus shalt thou say unto the children of Israel, I AM hath sent me unto you.

"GOD has spoken, were you, are you listening."

ROCK & FORTRESS

Psalm 31:3-5 (MSG)

You are my cave to hide in, my cliff to climb. Be my safe leader, be my true mountain guide. Free me from hidden traps; I want to hide in you. I've put my life in your hands. You won't drop me, you'll never let me down.

Rock: a symbol of God in the Old Testament. In Hebrew, the word is translated "mountain." Also translated as "rock," in Habakkuk 1:12- The "rock" from which the stone is cut there signifies the divine origin of Christ.

Christ as the Rock Defined: a person, suggesting a rock, especially in being dependable, unchanging, or providing firm foundation.

Fortress: any place of exceptional security; stronghold.

Safe, I heard it, did you? In case you missed it, I will say it again **S-A-F-E** that is correct. The Lord God has declared you as safe from hell and its stinky schemes. In fact He has given you a safe house to hide in times of trouble, and that place is in the heart of Himself. Can you really think of a safer place to bury you and your nuisances, irritations, struggles or heartaches in chaotic storms? I cannot, nor do I wish to think on the matter too long. My mother would say, "God said it and that settles it." Fortress: an exceptional place of security another way of saying extraordinarily unusual, which is funny. Let's say that we could come up with some of our own hiding places that we think may be safe. Could our mustered up, underground impervious abode really keep us out of harm's way? When I am like the scripture states above, on the cliff of a mountain; can it keep me from falling? Will the Shack that I erected be free from hidden traps? I do not think it is at all possible. So let us be sure to keep our lives in His hands; they are big hands so you and all your disorders, along with afflictions can fit too.

"My safe house is a ***Fortress*** *made complete,*
given by the solid ***Rock.****"*
"The ***Rock*** *has prepared a* ***Fortress*** *for me where I am Safe."*

WHO IS THIS GOD

Psalm 139:2-5 (CEV)

You know when I am resting, or when I am working, and from heaven, you discover my thoughts. You notice everything I do, and everywhere I go. Before I even speak a word, you know what I will say, and with your powerful arm, you protect me from every side.

Who is this God? He is Omniscient. He knows my thoughts afar off, in fact He knows before I do. His knowledge is infinite, and unlearned: this knowledge can never be seized. He knows us better than we know ourselves.

Malachi 3:6 (KJV)

For I am the LORD, I change not;
therefore ye sons of Jacob are not consumed

Who is this God? He is *Immutable,* He changes not. He is the same today, yesterday, will be the same tomorrow, and shall remain just Himself forevermore. His Word He declared is above His name. His very existence has remained unchangeable and unchanged.

Jeremiah 23:24 (KJV)

Can any hide himself in secret places that I shall not see him? saith the LORD. Do not I fill heaven and earth? saith the LORD

Who is this God? He is Omnipresent. He is everywhere present at all times. Time and space have never been able to hold Him. They too, are in His hands. He is both simultaneously animated and universal. In other words, He is coexistent, and unrestricted.

Job 42:2 (NKJV)

"I know that You can do everything,
And that no purpose *of Yours* can be withheld from You.

Who is this God? He is *Omnipotent.* His power is endless and all things in the heavens and earth stand because He is. Without His power, nothing could exist or remain constant or consistent. His omnipotence is under His holy and wise will.

Who is this GOD?

"He is Omniscient, He is Omnipresent, He is Omnipotent, and He is Immutable."

A SOWER

Matthew 13:37 (ESV)

Jesus answered: The one who scattered the good seed is the Son of Man.

Spring time is here, birds chirping, squirrels scrambling, bumble-bees pollinating and the butterflies are dancing in mid-air - all in celebration of the spring's glory. However, we humans have a different plight. We begin to read our flower seed instructions and hurry to the nearest mound of dirt with gardening tools in hand: ready to be one with the earth. Though I do not profess to have a green thumb, I do love nature and all that it's beauty affords. I have a confession; I have been gardening since childhood. However, for some odd reason, I could never remember the distinct difference between perennial or annual seeds. I assumed that because the name "annual" was most commonly used in terms like yearly events. Boy was I wrong! For me, gardening is special because I consider it to be me and Poppa's{GOD}time. Therefore, when I feel a sudden urgency to go planting, I hurry to the nearest flower bed in my yard with great anticipation knowing in any moment He will speak. Many of the revelations that I have written were a result of me playing in the dirt. Here is one for example: The word perennial is defined as perpetual, everlasting, continuing, recurrent, and able to reproduce. The seed is the Word of God. Jesus Christ, our perfect perennial seed, has sown the Word of truth in the hearts of all men. This gospel seed we offer to one another is a good seed that is certain to grow for generations. Therefore, stating this truth, when we plant this seed one to another, lives are forever transformed. Annual is defined as: living or lasting but one season or year, short lived. It cannot re-seed or reproduce. Look closely at this bogus annual seed (Satan), his time is short lived. He cannot reproduce from himself. And because he knows his time is only but for a season that will soon end, he contends daily against us. So if by any chance, you were like me, confused each new planting season not knowing which seed was certain to come back year after year. I pray this revelation helps you. Jesus Christ is the perennial seed that lives forever. He is always producing a life full of beautiful splendor in all seasons; in the garden of life.

"His unique seed is the only seed that can be planted in any season."

ARE YOU THAT SLEEPY?

Mark 11:34 & Mark 11:37-38 (NCV)

He said to them, "My heart is full of sorrow, to the point of death. Stay here and watch."
"Then Jesus went back to his followers and found them asleep.
He said to Peter, "Simon, are you sleeping? Couldn't you
stay awake with me for one hour? Stay awake and
pray for strength against temptation. The spirit wants to do what is right, but the body is weak."

OK. So, did the disciples really miss this sound counsel from the One who knew what was coming? My goodness! I know they had a long day. They had practically walked all over Jerusalem, witnessed Jesus curse a tree to its roots, and learned the greatest commandment; *love*. They were schooled on taxes, had dinner with Jesus' friend Simon of Bethany, and saw the Master's feet washed with expensive perfume. The disciples watched one of their friends betray them all. But most importantly, they had communion, the Last Supper. Why were they so tired? I would like to go here for a moment. Their great friend had informed them that men were coming to put Him to death. How could they think about sleeping at a time like this? They had witnessed Jesus' great works, and known Him to be trustworthy. Therefore, when He instructed them to pray, it was for their own good, and not His! I wonder if they had followed this great advice, would they have scattered. Well, I know that it really happened that way, all for the purposes of fulfilling scripture. However, I decree and declare that I will often pray so that the enemy that seeks my soul will have a harder time convincing me to fall into temptation.

"Not too sleepy to pray, well ponder this….
you may rest better if you pray first."

GOD IS CALLING

Acts 2:38-39 (KJV)

Then Peter said unto them, Repent, and be baptized every one of you in the name of Jesus Christ for the remission of sins, and ye shall receive the gift of the Holy Ghost.

For the promise is unto you, and to your children, and to all that are afar off, even as many as the LORD our God shall call.

Point blank, you could not save yourselves; your ability to have salvation is straightforward. **REPENT**. Once we take the responsibility to welcome the call for remission of our sins, we are now in the God family with great life benefits. The Holy Spirit is the fundamental component of our salvation plan; it is the Holy Spirit that reveals the Father and the Son to us. He is God indwelling us as the redeemed, therefore working within us to fulfill God's ultimate plan for our lives. There are 3 personal attributes to the Holy Spirit; He has a mind, a will, and emotions. This explains why He can be grieved, insulted, lied to, resisted, and even quenched if the full revelation of the Holy Spirit has not been completely or thoroughly acquired. We have access to God through Jesus by the Spirit. He is our go-between. God set us up for success in our salvation by offering us such a gift. He, by way of the Holy Spirit, makes His very presence known. The Holy Spirit teaches, guides, convicts, enables us to pray, and empowers us to witness to others so that they may come to Christ. He grants us spiritual gifts as He wills for the purposes of His kingdom. Can you imagine for a moment what your life would look like without this gift? Let me paint a picture: all hell would be loosed, and all evil would prevail. The plots the enemy devised would reign. Lastly, there would be a life of torment completely without peace, blessings, grace and mercy.

God called, answer……because it's your call for destiny and life.

"The Holy Spirit enables us to triumph in the life God designed."

THIS IS WHO HE

Mark 12:29 (ESV)

Jesus answered, "The most important is, 'Hear, O Israel: The Lord our God, the Lord is one.

Our God is the Father in all the fullness of the Godhead, invisible, without form, who no man, woman, boy, or girl has seen or can see. Nevertheless, HE is GOD.

He is the eternal Father.

He is our foundation of redemption: He decreed it and Jesus Christ fulfilled it.

He is Omnipresent, Omniscient, Omnipotent, Immutable and He is Eternal.

He is the covenant keeper of all ages.

He is Love, Light, and He is Life.

He is the sole designer, creator of the Heavens and the Earth.

He is the Perfection of Holiness, Perfect in Righteousness, and Perfecto in Faithfulness.

He is, according to Isaiah 43:10 (KJV), Ye are my witnesses, saith the LORD, and my servant whom I have chosen: that ye may know and believe me, and understand that I am he: before me there was no God formed, neither shall there be after me.

He is the ultimate Promise Keeper, always keeping His Word.

He is the ONE who hears & answers our prayers.

He is the ONE who has a Plan written for our lives.

He is the ONE who walked our days from End to Beginning.

He is not limited by time, and time does not hold Him. Yet, He holds all time in His hands.

He exists in Eternity & Eternity can only exist because He does.

"He is incomprehensible, He is invincible, and He is irresistible."

EPISODE TWO

OH, WHAT A GRACIOUS GOD

Genesis 1:21 (ESV)

So God created the great sea creatures and every living creature that moves, with which the waters swarm, according to their kinds, and every winged bird according to its kind. And God saw that it was good.

GRACIOUS

WHAT A GRACIOUS GOD

30 SECONDS WITHOUT

OUT OF THE MOUTH OF A BABE

HUMAN LOVE LETTER

NUMBERED

NOT SCARED

THE COWARD IN FEAR

ABOVE THY NAME

THY LOVING KINDNESS

PROVISION FOR MOMMA EEMA

GRACIOUS

Joel 2:13 (NIV)

Rend your heart, and not your garments. Return to the LORD your God, for he is gracious and compassionate, slow to anger and abounding in love, and he relents from sending calamity.

1 Peter 2:3

if indeed you have tasted that the Lord is gracious.

Exodus 33:19 (NKJV)

Then He said, "I will make all My goodness pass before you,
and I will proclaim the name of the LORD before you.
I will be gracious to whom I will be gracious, and I will have compassion on whom I will have compassion

Gracious: accommodating, affable, amiable, amicable, approachable, beneficent, **benevolent**, benign, benignant, big-hearted, bland, charitable, chivalrous, civil, **compassionate,** complaisant, congenial, considerate, cordial, courteous, courtly, easy, forthcoming, friendly, gallant, genial, good-hearted, good-natured, hospitable, indulgent, **lenient**, loving, merciful, mild, obliging, pleasing, polite, sociable, stately, suave, tender, unctuous, urbane, well-mannered. Where shall we begin? Which word puts the noted scripture in full perspective for you?

My choice - **lenient** - what I hear from this scripture is our Lord agrees with Himself on our behalf not to strike us down even though we know we deserved it. To have such attributes states He is agreeably tolerant. God, in all His stately grandeur, chooses to restrain His sovereign prerogative to execute judgment towards us. God is reluctant to punish. God in His divine nature has made it possible for the believer to experience His Grace and Compassion!

"O what a Benevolent God."

WHAT A GRACIOUS GOD!

Exodus 34:6 (NIV)

And he passed in front of Moses, proclaiming, "The LORD, the LORD, the compassionate and gracious God, slow to anger, abounding in love and faithfulness,

Psalm 111:4 (NIV)

He has caused his wonders to be remembered;
the LORD is gracious and compassionate.

Malachi 1:9 (NIV)

"Now plead with God to be gracious to us. With such offerings from your hands, will he accept you?"—says the LORD Almighty.

Isaiah 30:18 (MSG)

But God's not finished. He's waiting around to be gracious to you.
He's gathering strength to show mercy to you.
God takes the time to do everything right—everything.
Those who wait around for him are the lucky ones.

Numbers 6:25 (NKJV)

The LORD make His face shine upon you,
And be gracious to you;

Psalm 77:9 (NKJV)

Has His mercy ceased forever?
Has *His* promise failed forevermore?
Has God forgotten to be gracious?
Has He in anger shut up His tender mercies? Selah

Episode Two ~ Oh, What A Gracious God

Psalm 145:8 (NKJV)

The LORD *is* gracious and full of compassion,
Slow to anger and great in mercy.

"Chivalry is not dead; it has a different swagger today ...called Grace."

30 SECONDS WITHOUT

Romans 5:17 (NKJV)

For if by the one man's offense death reigned through the one, much more those who receive abundance of grace and of the gift of righteousness will reign in life through the One, Jesus Christ.)

I recently posted on my Facebook™ page, "We are not perfect: just Christians that are saved by a **PERFECT GOD** that is it, that is all." Within seconds after the post several people hit the "Like" button. Some posted a Comment which read like, "I so needed that!" Then, another wrote, "I am so hard on myself, so this reminder was timely." I responded back to the first two comments. My first reply, "Now you got it walk it out," and my second response, "While in prayer, the Lord spoke these very words to me. "We are not perfect just forgiven **and** saved by a perfect GOD." The devil is such a liar; it is God's grace that keeps us together: no more or any less. Go here with me just for a moment. Imagine what your life would be if there were just 30 seconds without the Father's grace on your life……What a scary thought? Right? The grace that has been attached to our lives by way of the blood keeps us from things seen and un-seen. If you ponder a moment, those things in which you know you witnessed with your eyes that will put praise in your mouth, and a dance in your feet. What kind of praise could there be if we saw the dangers, trials, or tragedies that He has kept far from us? In most cases, we usually put ourselves in the dilemmas that we now need to be rescued from? I must caution you to remember that you and I are not perfect: just forgiven and saved by a perfect God. He is always there with the adequate grace needed for this not so perfect Christian. So admonish yourself, as instructed through scripture. "Encourage your own self in the Lord." Do like David when the battle raged against him because he knew who he was and who's he was, perfection was not his goal, acknowledging the grace he had was. So, the next time guilt wants to take you out, say this and keep it moving, "I am not perfect." I am a work-in-progress, being perfected by the blood works of Calvary, by a most Holy, sovereign, and righteous God: that will, in the end, complete His perfected & original plan in our lives. So, devil shut-up!!!

"Cannot imagine 30 Seconds without it… Grace"

OUT OF THE MOUTH OF A BABE

Matthew 21:16 (AMP)

And they said to Him, Do You hear what these are saying? And Jesus replied to them, Yes; have you never read, Out of the mouths of babes and unweaned infants You have made (provided) perfect praise?

While sitting at the park, I watched the children run, swing, slide their little bodies down the slide. However there are some playing in the grass - - only to get itchy skin. All of a sudden I hear these little voices shout, "ice cream truck!" Amidst all of the above fun, the kids stop and scurry over a tasty, treat. The ice cream truck has music for children's ears, "Puff the Magic Dragon," to be exact. As I'm watching these children play, I am wonderfully reminded of an event I recently attended. Shortly after the release of my 1st book to this series, my publisher, editor and I were invited to a book club. The ladies were reading the book, "The Shack" by William Paul Young. My editor and I are not just business partners, but also teachers in the same ministry, as well as dear friends. The amusement here is that "The Shack" just also happens to be one of our favorite books. We had just taught, "The Shack" to our women's book club at our church. This time of fellowship was both an honor as well as a treat. But, little did I know much more would transpire for moi on this interesting evening? I am certain God orchestrated such events for reasons I believe to settle my doubt as He was probably fatigued with me asking, "Are you sure this is what I have been called to do?" I bet you ask Him similar questions pertaining to where you are right now. The evening became more special, when out of the mouth of a babe; my life took an affirmed turn in the right direction. Her name was Bree-On, and asked for my autograph. There were only two children at this intimate event. I must admit that's not why I recall her or the moment so well. However, it is because I'd been observing her and her sister that night. And from time to time, I watched them as they would pass through to chat with the woman sitting next to me. I would later learn was their mother. At one point, I noticed the youngest of the two had her boots on the wrong feet, which made me chuckle. After speaking, I was asked to sign books. And while signing and chatting with these amazing women, somewhere in the room, I hear a little whisper. She said, “Mommy what’s going on? The mother replied in that same monotone whisper, "That woman sitting there is a writer. She wrote the book we have been discussing." In a breathy gasp, I witnessed that same excitement I heard when the children shouted "ice cream truck!" But, she was not shouting about ice cream. This little girl was referring to my book. She said, "Mommy I need a pen! Quick! To get my 1st famous person’s autograph." I was doing my best to keep my composure. Moments later, she appeared in front of me, attempting to stand eye-level to my face. Asking with her sweet voice, "Can I have your autograph?" Holding back my tears in this life-altering wink, **I replied** "who should I sign this to?" Innocently she replied, B r e e dash-O n. I wrote just as she asked. This moment was priceless! She pranced off to her mother cheering, "I got it! I got it! My 1st famous person’s autograph." I know I'm not famous, yet I have been called to write witty & creative thoughts, based on facts about our Lord. I believe HE wanted me to stop asking, “Are You sure?” So, like the scripture states above, out of the mouth of a babe, He spoke.

“Innocent Words of praise fall from the lips of babes……LISTEN.”

HUMAN LOVE LETTER

2 Corinthians 3:3-6 (MSG)

Your very lives are a letter that anyone can read by just looking at you. Christ himself wrote it—not with ink, but with God's living Spirit; not chiseled into stone, but carved into human lives— and we publish it.
We couldn't be more sure of ourselves in this—that you, written by Christ himself for God, are our letter of recommendation. We wouldn't think of writing this kind of letter about ourselves Only God can write such a letter.

I scurry to the mailbox to see if my true love has sent me a few sweet nothings by mail; a card or maybe a precious, "I can't live without your promise note." Remember the days of your first crush? You would doodle your name next to theirs inside of a big red heart. Perhaps you came from the era where it was the flower petals pulled one-by-one. "He loves me! He loves me not." But, if the last petal pulled landed on "loves me not petal," then you chose another flower from the garden nearby - only to start over again. I propose to you that there has been two love letters written for our gleaning. Or, should we say, earthly recommendation. First, Christ's love letter to us written by God alone, not written in ink as noted in the scripture above, however, it is written by the spirit of His Father. We read in the Word that He clearly endorsed for our living. The second is the love letter, He has given us to show others as a way to Him. The recipient can only read this letter as we demonstrate it through our very lives. We ensure the proper delivery when we motivate the admirer to search for more letters through the word we once read as the receiver. Would you agree that when you came into salvation it was as a result of two important events? #1 You were sought out by the Father, #2 God allowed you to read someone else's letter so you could come to know His love, which is never matched in human ways. Well my human love letter, you are the love letter someone needs to read. His letter authorizes us to help carry out this new plan of action. The plan was not written with ink on pages and pages with legal footnotes- killing your spirit. Rather, it is written with Spirit-on-spirit. His life on our lives!

Hurry to the mailbox...
Will you be the recipient or the deliverer?

NUMBERED

Luke 12:7 (ESV)

Why, even the hairs of your head are all numbered. Fear not; you are of more value than many sparrows.

Just a fraction of His goodness is noted in this declaration. WOW! do you ever find yourself truly pondering over His absolute commitment to you? If your answer is "yes," are you overwhelmed by it? Sincerely stating that the hairs on our head are numbered, which means when we see our hair in our comb or brush it's just hairs to us. but God says, "That was strand number "three or seven." Awesome right? His design is much like a blueprint with a strategic outline. Such insightful concepts allow me to know that not only does my life have purpose, it also has significance. I don't consider it a light thing that He not only gave me life but I was also granted the opportunity to get to know my personal designer. If you are a Vera Wang™ or Sean Jean™ fan, then you often purchase the latest fashion haute couture. But think about it. Have you ever had the chance to meet designers of the attire you quickly ran out to buy so this style could adorn your physique? By now, you are probably saying, "Oh my goodness! What's with all the questions?" My answer is simple. I just want you to take note that your original designer has no notes to refer to, or specs to consider. When it comes down to us, His personal plan and purpose as to why He created you in the first place is sufficient. God the Father is so in tune with us. He makes our importance to Him clear. I am willing to bet that when I change my nail polish today, He knew what color I'd chose before I did. Just like when I brushed my hair today and saw tresses in the brush. I don't know what numbers they were, I just know there were a few. When you lose a button or your zipper loosens from its fashionable design, do you think Vera Wang or Sean Jean know which lot it's from?

"Brushing my hair today I lost a few hairs,
God what numbers were they?"

NOT SCARED

Isaiah 41:10 (ESV)

fear not, for I am with you; be not dismayed, for I am your God; I will strengthen you, I will help you, I will uphold you with my righteous right hand.

Scared of what? With certainty, we can rest assured if God says there is nothing for us to fear, He means just that. He will contend with those that rise up against us: it's a fixed fight. Believe me; I know that there are circumstances that will cause our knees to tremble. Oftentimes, even those times happen to those of us that appear to be strong, tough, and enduring. In the book of Isaiah 43:1-2, the Lord declares that because He created us, He promises to keep us no matter the condition. However, we must be obedient to the destiny He planned for us. Look at Jonah. All he needed to do was go to Nineveh as the Father ordered. Once he conceded, tout de suite! The fish had to cough him up - not in the sea, but back onto dry land. God also promised that when we walk through the waters, He would be there. How else did the children of Israel get to the other side? Not only did He part the Red Sea for the Israelites, but just like He promised, God would make away of escape for us. He set them free from the hands of the Egyptians (their enemy). Lastly, I must boast of one more generous fact about the God that He pursued us. He is just: whatever He promises or does for one of His children, He will certainly do it again for another. Shadrach, Meshach and Abednego were thrown in the fire because King Nebuchadnezzar was upset that these three boys refused to worship an image of gold. It's height was sixty cubits and its breadth was six cubits. King Nebuchadnezzar had them thrown into a fiery furnace which he ordered to be turned up seven times greater than ever before. The three boys remembered that God himself promised, "When you walk through fire you shall not be burned; and the flame shall not consume you." Not only did God deliver them; they walked away without even the smell of smoke on their garments! Yes, I believe He is a promise keeper! SCARED? No! FEARFUL? Nope! SHAKEN? Not even stirred.

"Trembling knees should bend in preparation of prayer to witness a Miracle."

THE COWARD IN FEAR

Psalms 55:4-7 (AMP)

My heart is grievously pained within me, and the terrors of death have fallen upon me.

If the truth be told there is a little coward in all of us. The irony about this bully in us is that we are unaware of this little feeble part of our being. That is, until the proper situation presents itself. Otherwise, we are giving the best advice to those around us needing a simple push, a few prayers, or maybe just a shoulder to lean on for a little encouragement. Then, the table turns, your boat is rocked: you do not even remember how to use the sail for proper direction. Let alone, remember where the anchor is located. For a split second you forget you have a CB radio and how quickly you can connect with the Coast Guard. Once you reach them, your safety becomes their priority. However, the moment information is transmitted from your head to your heart, panic sets in. All of your nautical wits are gone. Let me encourage you with another verifiable truth, your boat is sailing on seas created by the ONE who desires to love & keep you safe.

"Tossed to-&-fro, your ship does not have to dock here....press."

ABOVE THY NAME

Psalms 138:2 (KJV)

I will worship toward thy holy temple, and praise thy name for thy loving kindness and for thy truth: for thou hast magnified thy word above all thy name.

It is impossible to put the inspired, infallible Word of God on too high a pedestal, for God Himself honors it above His name! The Word is not greater than God is for He wrote it by His Spirit, but it is greater than His name, which represents Him, and all that He is and does. The Word in fact is His name revealed. The name of the Lord refers to the manifestation of His character and nature. God's Word refers to His promises to us, when others see these promises (prayer) answered His name is exalted and He yet again is glorified in the earth. The WORD of God is good for doctrine, reproof, and correction, which is in righteousness for the purposes of God speaking on His own behalf to us for Him for our good and for the good of those around us. Also, look at this great truth, **John 1:1-2(NKJV) In the beginning was the Word, and the Word was with God, and the Word was God. He was in the beginning with God**. God is clearly stating that His only begotten Son He has put above His own Name, Jesus is the Word as it states above. The creator of it all has made it plain just how much Jesus means to Him and this should matter to us. Consider how many names of God there are I have found over 625 and in this verse He declares that He has personally put His Word above all of them. Just to give you a glimpse at a few of the many names in hope that you will see just how extensive this declaration is; Elohim the self existing one, Adonai Lord and Master, Nissi our banner, Jireh our provider, Shalom our peace, Tsidkenu our righteousness, Rohi our shepherd just to name a few. The remarkable thing about this is that all of these names again make up for every scripture verse you will ever read. Again, His Word reveals His name, concluding that the self-existing one that is our Lord and Master is our true banner that provides peace coupled with righteousness. Yes He is the good Shepherd. Magnified above all this, I too will worship toward His holy temple and praise His name for His loving kindness and for His truth.

"This settles it His Word is above His Name."
or
It is settled His Word is above His Name

THY LOVING KINDNESS

Psalm 63:3 (KJV)

Because thy loving-kindness is better than life,
my lips shall praise thee.

Psalm 63:3 (MSG)

So here I am in the place of worship, eyes open, drinking in your strength and glory. In your generous love I am really living at last! My lips brim praises like fountains. I bless you every time I take a breath; My arms wave like banners of praise to you

Loving-Kindness; tender kindness motivated by or expressing affection.

David expresses to God in the wilderness that he is thirsty. He is lonely. He exclaims that, "God's love is far better than life itself." David had relationship with the Father. And for this reason, he could proclaim, "My lips shall praise thee." Tender is so apropos when carefully placed in conjunction with our Lord. Tender denotes delicate, soft, in no ways tough. However, it is considerably careful and compassionate. God's loving-kindness is truly what motivated His ultimate expression of affection when He put in place a strategy for our living eternally. Jesus sheds His blood on the cross, while we were yet still in our sinful state. David had experience with God, so he could say with conviction. "I would rather praise You in the state I am in, than have to live without you. Solomon had the same affection toward God when he responded in Lamentations 3:23, "Great is thy faithfulness." Great are Your tender affections toward me. So, like David and Solomon, I make this my declaration, Lord God of heaven, I thank You for Your loving-kindness and Your tender mercies I see with the rising of Your *Son* each day.

Lord you alone are worthy of the fruit of my lips, your loving-kindness motivates my PRAISE."

PROVISIONS FOR EEMA אמא

(Mom in Hebrew)

John 19:25-27 (NKJV)

Now there stood by the cross of Jesus His mother, and His mother's sister, Mary the wife of Clopas, and Mary Magdalene. When Jesus therefore saw His mother, and the disciple whom He loved standing by, He said to His mother, "Woman, behold your son!" Then He said to the disciple, "Behold your mother!" And from that hour that disciple took her to his own home.

"What a Son!" I could hear Mary say sometimes to herself and possibly to others close in her company. Consider Jesus as your perfect child, teenager, and a young man. Imagine if you can, the entries in Mary's daily journals from the moment the angel came to tell her the exciting news: she would carry the Messiah. Mary's mind fast-forwards to when she would see Joseph, her fiancés face, once he was told she is carrying a babe in her womb. After all, she was a *VIRGIN,* what story could she muster up? Nevertheless, for the moment our concern is not Joseph. Instead, let us focus our hearts on her anointed Son, whose name she will call Emmanuel. Many mothers pray for their children, as well as they pray that they will be all that God desires them to be as parents. What about when you are the mother of God? Then what? Jesus was an obedient son both to His natural parents and of course to His heavenly Father. This further explains why He was such a perfect Son. However, an incident occurred when Jesus was 12, and traveling to Jerusalem with His parents for the Passover feast. He lagged behind when they were to return home. When Mary and Joseph returned back in Jerusalem to get Him, Jesus replied, "Why did you seek Me? Did you not know that I must be about My Father's business?" They did not understand the statement which He spoke to them. Then He went down with them and came to Nazareth, and was subject to them. But His mother kept all these things in her heart. He understood that while He had authority being born the Savior,

He was still a child subject to His parents' order. Jesus worked alongside Joseph as a carpenter. Later this was His means to support His mother after Joseph's death. Then there was the wedding in Galilee. Mary approaches her Son, "they have no more wine." It is just like a mother to try to help what she can within her means, in this case her means as well as ours is Jesus. However, Jesus knowing His time has not yet come turns the water into wine then states this, "Draw *some water* out now, and take *it* to the master of the feast," and they took *it*. What a Son! What pain she must have felt in her heart that gruesome day at the cross. Mary witnessed her perfect Son scourged, spit upon, slandered, mocked, betrayed, and then put to death. Nevertheless, Jesus being this great *Son* was not finished with His earthly provisions for Momma. Jesus, this final earthly provision, was to ensure that Mary was taken care of even during His death at the Cross!

"Jesus' death also provided His Eema eternal life, for the life she gave this perfect Son."

EPISODE THREE

HOW MUCH DID IT COST?

2 Corinthians 9:8 (NKJV)

And God is able to make all grace abound toward you, that you, always having all sufficiency in all things, may have an abundance for every good work.

BLOOD ~ SWEAT ~ TEARS

Luke 22:42-44 (ESV)

Jesus saying, "Father, if you are willing, remove this cup from me. Nevertheless, not my will, but yours, be done." And there appeared to him an angel from heaven, strengthening him. And being in an agony he prayed more earnestly; and his sweat became like great drops of blood falling down to the ground.

Who would ever imagine that the Son of God had such anguish for the task set before Him? Jesus, fully aware that He was born to die, did not annul the fact that He was still a human being with feelings much like our own. You must understand that even though He was the Christ, and for this reason He came. Who in any form naturally or spiritually, welcomes suffering? In this case, Jesus in His humanity expressed dread, which was His true feelings about the coming agony and trial that He would endure: to secure our salvation. Nevertheless, He was still committed to follow the plans of His Father before the world began. When Jesus spoke of the cup, He was not referring to the pain, agony and tears of blood dripping down His face. What really grieved Him was the total separation He would experience from His Heavenly Father: after our sin was accounted to Him! Jesus had never been without the divine presence of His Father. Such separation to Him was worse than the crucifixion itself. He said, "Nevertheless, not my will….." The bottom line: He was obedient unto the death of the cross. Even though it cost Him blood, sweat, and tears! To further bring this revelation to light: on the cross. is the first time in scripture, where Jesus referred to His Father as God. (Mark 15:34 KJV). It says, "And at the ninth hour Jesus cried with a loud voice, saying, 'Eloi, Eloi, lama sabachthani?' Which is, interpreted, My God, my God, why hast thou forsaken me? Jesus called Him God, not Father. If we thought more like Jesus in our life's trials and became "nevertheless" Christians, I am certain our troubles would not last as long. Our Heavenly just as He did for Jesus, will give us more grace to endure life's challenges. My mother use to say when we would come to her with the problems that I now understand were "trivial," "Well, at least you did not have to endure the cross." I understand the necessary truth and relationship today as I scribe this devotion. Part of me believes that perhaps this is what she was saying, "Be grateful because your minuscule circumstance didn't in no ways separate you from the Father in Heaven."

Amidst all the blood, sweat and tears that life will cause, are you a "Nevertheless" Christian?

HAD TO CONFESS

John 19:19-22 (KJV)

Pilate wrote a title, and put it on the cross. The writing was JESUS OF NAZARETH THE KING OF THE JEWS. This title then read many of the Jews: for the place where Jesus was crucified was nigh to the city: and it was written in Hebrew, and Greek, and Latin. Then said the chief priests of the Jews to Pilate, Write not, The King of the Jews; but that he said, I am King of the Jews.
Pilate answered, what I have written I have written.

Notice how Pilate was hesitant about putting this King to death. If you study the previous verses, before he wrote the sign he went back-and-forth, drilling questions that he, himself asked Jesus. I can imagine his face looking perplexed. Wrinkled forehead, eyebrows knit, and arms crossed when he asked Jesus in John 19:35, "What have you done?" Pilate, after his own assessment of Jesus found no fault in our Savior. Just in case you are looking for fault you will not find any today. The charges against Jesus were for confessing He was a King. Was Pilate trying to remember had he ever had such a case before? Was saying you were a King cause for death? They did not believe it to be true, however Pilate knew in his heart it was so. What other reason would he have written the sign in several languages for all to see?

Philippians 2:9-11 (MSG)

Because of that obedience, God lifted him high and honored him far beyond anyone or anything, ever, so that all created beings in heaven and on earth even those long ago dead and buried will bow in worship before this Jesus Christ, and call out in praise that he is the Master of all, to the glorious honor of God the Father.

John 18:37(KJV)

Pilate therefore said unto him, Art thou a king then? Jesus answered; Thou sayest that I am a king. To this end was I born, and for this cause came I into the world, that I should bear witness unto the truth. Every one that is of the truth heareth my voice.

When it comes to JESUS, we will all.......have to CONFESS!.....Selah

BLINDFOLDED

Luke 22:64 (NKJV)

And having blindfolded Him, they struck Him on the face and asked Him, saying, "Prophesy! Who is the one who struck You?"

On a flight traveling back from the East Coast I was excited. Because God always, and I mean ALWAYS speaks to me in my travels! I need to explain that I use to be afraid to fly. Today, I am no longer afraid. I understand why, because on airplanes I receive some good revelations. During this particular flight, I eagerly waited for the pilot to give us permission to turn on our computer gadgets. This meant we had reached an altitude that would not hinder the flight's necessary cockpit thingy's. Gazing out of my window, I noticed the tons of fluffy white cotton balls (clouds) suspended in mid-air. I thought, or should I say, the Holy Spirit said to me, "Even the clouds cannot obstruct His view." We cannot see past, above, or below the clouds. But He sees it all. The soldier that blindfolded Christ was not privy to such info. For if he had then he would have known that Christ knew exactly who slapped Him. And for that reason, He asked the Lord to forgive them. Maybe, he covered His eyes because he could not face Jesus. So he punked out! Think about it, when you are doing wrong don't you do it in the dark**?**

Mark 4:22 (NKJV)

For there is nothing hidden which will not be revealed, nor has anything been kept secret but that it should come to light.

"No Blindfold, not even the clouds can obstruct God's view."

IN THE MIDDLE

John 19:18 (TNIV)

Here they crucified him, and with him two others—one on each side and Jesus in the middle.

Have you ever wondered why Jesus was in the center of the two criminals? Think about it. There was a criminal on each side of Him that day on Calvary. At the onset, they both shouted slandering words. However, one reconsidered, and when this heart change took place, he asked that Jesus remember him in His kingdom. To take it a step further, this same robber rebuked the other criminal. Luke 23:39-43: But, the other criminal rebuked him. "Don't you fear God," he said, "Since you are under the same sentence? We are punished justly, for we are getting what our deeds deserve. But this man has done nothing wrong." Then he said, "Jesus, remember me when you come into your kingdom." Jesus answered him, "Truly I tell you, today you will be with me in paradise." Two things transpired here, the first thing, the one criminal admitted his guilt. Isn't this is what we are supposed to do in order to be forgiven? Secondly, Jesus proved to us yet again, that He takes us just as we are. My own heart theory is there is a particular reason Jesus was in the center. All that God does is on purpose. Therefore, having a great significance. The Father illustrates that because of the bloodshed that day on Calvary, Christ should forever be the CENTER of our lives. God could also, at this point of scripture, want to give us a visual scope as to what choice looks like. Judgment or forgiveness was given, both men were given the same opportunity to repent and accept Jesus as Lord. Nevertheless, only one recognized that the ONE that could grant such a pardon was right there next to him……in the *Middle.*

"In the middle for a Purpose……you Choose."

PURIFIED WATER

John 19:34 (KJV)

But, one of the soldiers with a spear pierced his side, and forthwith came there out blood and water.

Whether it is H20 or aqua, bottled, tap, distilled, filtered, or fountain. I think we can all agree that water is essential to our living. Studies have proven that the body can go for days, even weeks without food. However, without water, the body starts to shut down after 3 days. WOW! Jesus rose from the dead on the 3rd day. He was well-equipped for the task of delivering this water we needed. The Holy Spirit is the water I am referring to. Therefore, while the soldier did this to be certain that Christ was dead, in actuality he was doing his part to fulfill scripture. Look at this point in scripture written by John, since he among all the disciples was there to witness his Master's death; John 7:38-39. "Does anyone believe in me?" Then, just as Scripture says, "Streams of living water will flow from inside him." When He said this, He meant the Holy Spirit. Those who believed in Jesus would receive the Spirit later. Up to that time, the Spirit had not been given. This was because Jesus had not yet received glory. Jesus told the Samaritan woman in John 4:14, "But whoever drinks of the water that I shall give him will never thirst. But the water that I shall give him will become in him a fountain of water springing up into everlasting life." The blood was shed to save us and grants forgiveness for our sins. The blood is God's sacrifice for us. The water was given to assist us because we are just visitors in this natural world that have a supernatural part in our natural being. The water is God's spirit in us. Thank you, Jesus!

"Blood washed, my Thirst quenched."

THIS MOUNTAIN

Matthew 17:20 (NKJV)

So Jesus said to them, "Because of your unbelief; for assuredly, I say to you, if you have faith as a mustard seed, you will say to this mountain, 'Move from here to there,' and it will move; and nothing will be impossible for you.

Driving on highway 5 North through the grapevine pass, it is foggy with very low visibility, if you are not familiar with this terrain, it is best to travel when the fog has lifted. **Fog**: cloudlike mass or layer of minute water droplets or ice crystals near the surface of the earth, appreciably reducing visibility, to perplex or bewilder. This definition of fog sounds simple, however we all know that it is not. Mountains obstruct a few things in our lives, especially when we travel roads that are just not familiar to us. Think about it, if there is a curve where the dense layer appears, do you not tend to slow down? Well, slowing down takes wisdom, oftentimes depending on how low this misty mass is, the road you are on tends to be quite slippery. We should practice our mustard seed faith by stating this truth, once I get past this mountain it will clear up. Jesus said our faith could move mountains if we just believe, and when we do activate this precious mustard seed faith nothing will be impossible for us.

"Some mountains are critical for our faith to grow. So pace yourself and know once you get past it.....things will clear up."

B4 MEN

Matthew 10:33 (NCV)

But all who stand before others and say they do not believe in me, I will say before my Father in heaven that they do not belong to me.

Why suffer yourself? After tasting the goodness of the awesome Lord, why would anyone have the audacity to deny the One who actually gave you life? What benefit would such rejection grant? I remember writing a devotion titled, "No More Blood." This type of repudiate is in the same vein. Why would one risk such eternal damnation? So again, I ask. Why suffer yourself? There are so many mistakes that we can make that are forgivable. However, to deny Jesus is a sure way to get a one-way ticket to Hades. It is a questionless matter. After all, look at all He has done for us to obtain mercy and grace. His blood is the everlasting sacrifice! That is truly the only reason we are able to manage in the earth. Can you imagine your life without this blood securing your daily opportunity to get in His Father's face? I cannot! And, for the sake of your soul, I pray that neither can you. John scribed these words pertaining to what Jesus has done on our behalf; John 17:12 (NIV), "While I was with them, I protected them and kept them safe by that name you gave me. None has been lost except the one doomed to destruction so that Scripture would be fulfilled." Not one lost! WOW! That's a loyal commitment He has made for everyone. Don't you love Him for loving you that much? I would never want to be in the position where Jesus Christ, the one who gave me life from His life, to look at me in the presence of His Father and say_________________(your name) does not belong to me. So ask yourself is there any type of threat, persecution, scandal, or intimidation that would cause you to say "Jesus who"...?

"No disowning I herald today & forever B4 all men young & old…that. Jesus Christ is Lord."

YOUR *HIERON*

Greek translation for Temple

1 Corinthians 6:19-20 (AMP)

Do you not know that your body is the temple (the very sanctuary) of the Holy Spirit, Who lives within you, whom you have received [as a Gift] from God? You are not your own. You were bought with a price [purchased with preciousness and paid for, made His own]. So then, honor God and bring glory to Him in your body.

I see her at Trader Joes after there had been sometime between us. We use to work together when I was a manager for Victoria's Secret. She peeks into my basket and say's "looks like someone's on a diet, I said "just trying to get healthy" then you should give me a call this is my line of work. So the work begins, on a spring day in April that I must admit was life changing. Her name is Lisa, a tiny and very petite personal trainer, meets me for my assessment so that we can put a personal strategy in place for moi. The measurements all jotted down, my weight, my current diet, my personal objective as to why this was important to me at this season in my life. Was I doing it for me, or to impress other's i.e.: my husband, friends, children, etc? "No this is all for me to be a better and healthier me." "Great then you will succeed," her last and final question how much rest do you get daily? I was proud of my answer because my lack of rest was due to my writing frenzy to complete the series, Some Things Made Plain. "I average about 3-5 hours of sleep each day." Lisa looked at me as if I had told her a graphic horror story and replied "**your poor *TEMPLE.*"** My heart raced, my mind went right to the above scripture. I remembered all that has been written aforetime, was written for our learning (Romans 15:4), gulp, gasp, sigh, and repent. I have been in violation to my precious tenant, the Holy Spirit. The 20th verse makes apparent the importance of following such warning, our temples have been *"bought at a price,"* refers to slaves purchased at an auction. Christ's death freed us from sin, the cross indebts us to His service; if you live in a building owned by someone, you do your best not to violate the owner's rules? This should wake us up and give full revelation that our bodies are not our own, they belong to God, so lets start living by His standards. Paul told the believers that each one of their bodies was a *naos, a sanctuary for God.* Paul also said that the church, as Christ's body, is a spiritual temple for God. What a special privilege it is to be God's dwelling place both individually and corporately.

"This tenant is ONE tenant you want to for Life".

HOLY MANIFESTATION

John 1:14 (KJV)

And the Word was made flesh, and dwelt among us, (and we beheld his glory, the glory as of the only begotten of the Father,) full of grace and truth.

John 1:14 (AMP)

And the Word (Christ) became flesh (human, incarnate) and tabernacled (fixed His tent of flesh, lived awhile) among us; and we [actually] saw His glory (His honor, His majesty), such glory as an only begotten son receives from his father, full of grace (favor, loving-kindness) and truth.

In the beginning was the Word, and the Word was with God, and the Word was God. The same was in the beginning with God. That is scripture, but let's say it this way. In the beginning was Jesus, and Jesus was with God, and Jesus is God. Jesus was in the beginning with God. Some of you may be saying, "Duh." Then, others may disagree, whatever your stance is, my heart says this Jesus, has been here all along. However, let us go a little deeper. God became a man all to die for you and me. The Son of God who was from eternity became flesh, with limitations in time and space, while Christ became *flesh* nothing in His essential nature of His deity was lost. He was and is GOD. Remember when God revealed Himself to Moses. In Exodus 34:6, And the LORD passed by before him, and proclaimed, The LORD, The LORD God, merciful and gracious, longsuffering, and abundant in goodness and truth? This can be an applied fact, that the life of Jesus Christ manifested for us perfect redemption, and perfect revelation. Grace for Grace His love for us manifests unmerited favor. His abundant goodness is His love for us that is why He was born to die.

Grace: Romans 3:24 (AMP) [All] are justified and made upright and in right standing with God, freely and gratuitously by His grace (His unmerited favor and mercy), through the redemption which is [provided] in Christ Jesus,

Truth: *John 14:6, Jesus said to him, I am the Way and the Truth and the Life; no one comes to the Father except by (through) Me.*

"Life was not created, life existed in Christ."

NOW THAT'S GOOD

Psalm 52:9 (AMP)

I will thank You and confide in You forever, because You have done it [delivered me and kept me safe]. I will wait on, hope in and expect in Your name, for it is ***good****, in the presence of Your saints (Your kind and pious ones).*

Good: Excellent; virtuous; morally good; and pious.
A **good** Man

And God saw that the light was good (suitable, pleasant) and He approved it; and God separated the light from the darkness.

God called the dry land Earth, and the accumulated waters He called Seas. And God saw that this was good (fitting, admirable) and He approved it.

The earth brought forth vegetation: plants, yielding seeds, according to their own kinds. Trees bearing fruit in which was their seed, each according to its kind. And God saw that it was good (suitable, admirable) and He approved it.

To rule over the day and night, and to separate the light from the darkness. And God saw that it was good (fitting, pleasant) and He approved it.

God created the great sea monsters and every living creature that moves which the waters brought forth abundantly, according to their kind; and every winged bird according to its kind. And God saw that it was good (suitable, admirable) and He approved it.

God made the [wild] beasts of the earth, according to their kind, and domestic animals according to their kind, and everything that creeps upon the earth according to its kind. And God saw that it was good (fitting, pleasant), and He approved it.

"God saw that all He made was good. Well you are a part of God's creation. I am certain He is pleased when He looks in your direction, He says, Now That's Good."

FROM HELL TO GLORY

Matthew 12:40 (NKJV)

For as Jonah was three days and three nights in the belly of the great fish, so will the Son of Man be three days and three nights in the heart of the earth.

The Calvary Tribune's top headline story in Jerusalem might have read something like this on its front page; "The King of the Jews was crucified today on Golgotha Hill! Witnesses say that when Jesus Christ took His last breath, the skies went dark, rocks split, and there was a sudden earthquake!" Could it be that the earth shook in this manner? As the scripture states above, the Son of Man spent 3 days in the heart of the earth (HELL). Did the earth shake in this manner because its creator was coming in, and hell itself could not contain His grand size? Christ as Savior had a purpose for us all. **1 Peter 3:18-19 (AMP):** For Christ [the Messiah Himself] died for sins once and for all, the Righteous for the unrighteous (the Just for the unjust, the Innocent for the guilty), that He might bring us to God. In His human body, was put to death, but He was made alive in the spirit, in which He went and preached to the spirits in prison. Jesus was in hell ministering to them that had died before the dispensation of *Grace. Jesus was born to die.*

God's perfect will for us is that none of His children should perish, therefore in His sovereignty Jesus made His way to Hades to minister to them that were lost before His blood hit the mercy seat. **John 20:17 (KJV):** Jesus saith unto her, Touch me not; for I am not yet ascended to my Father: but go to my brethren, and say unto them, I ascend unto my Father, and your Father; and to my God, and your God. Jesus was telling Mary, "My Blood has not yet hit the mercy seat. I still have work to do. Your clinging to me will hold up the process and I must do this in order for my Spirit, the Holy Spirit, to come." The Spirit assists us in the work that still needs to be done for God's Kingdom.

"The mercy seat made all things Possible for us."

EPISODE FOUR

FAVOR FACTOR

Matthew 16:18 (NKJV)

And I also say to you that you are Peter, and on this rock I will build My church, and the gates of Hades shall not prevail against it.

THE GRACE GIFT

ADJUSTMENTS IN TURBULENCE

THIS IS LOVE

WE ARE HEALED

HOLY GHOST BUILT

NO COMPARISON

NOT ASHAMED

FELT IMPOSSIBLE

AU NATUREL SCAMPER

THE LAST 1ST

PROPHETIC FOUNDATION

THE GRACE GIFT

Ephesians 2:8 (AMP)

For it is by free grace (God's unmerited favor) that you are saved (delivered from judgment and made partakers of Christ's salvation) through [your] faith. And this [salvation] is not of yourselves [of your own doing, it came not through your own striving], but it is the gift of God;

No need to brag, and it is certainly not because you deserve it. But, My love for you outweighs any punishment that I could render. Instead, I purpose to give you a gift. I have pardoned you because of My blood at the cross. Think of it this way. In regards to that sin matter which has come to so easily beset you. Don't worry anymore about the one you keep asking for My forgiveness. I limit Myself daily when you ask for it, and splash unmerited favor in your direction.

Gift: something given voluntarily without payment in return, as to show favor toward someone, honor an occasion, or make a gesture of assistance; present.

Grace: the freely given, unmerited favor and love of God. The influence or spirit of God operating in humans to regenerate or strengthen them. A virtue or excellence of divine origin: the Christian graces.

Ephesians 4:7(HCSB): Now grace was given to each one of us according to the measure of the Messiah's gift.

This Grace gift has been measured by the Master Potter, individually and strategically based on the life He knew we would live. That's why He says

His grace is sufficient for what things may come. Our trials and tribulations have been measured and sealed in the blood, all for the sake of us being partakers of Christ's salvation. We are set free from the judgment that truly is warranted.

"Unwrapping my GRACE GIFT *and saying thank you Master, it's just what I needed."*

ADJUSTMENTS IN TURBULENCE

John 3:8 (NCV)

The wind blows where it wants to and you hear the sound of it, but you don't know where the wind comes from or where it is going. It is the same with every person who is born from the Spirit."

I remember a season when I experienced a phobia of flying. Turbulence was my fear factor. For some odd reason, I had in my mind that turbulence dictated the downright End! Satan is such a liar! Turbulence is an irregular motion of the atmosphere, as indicated by gusts and lulls in the wind. I would like to propose another way to look at the turbulence. It comes to grow us. The Holy Spirit in Greek is translated to: "Wind," the life-giving breath of God in its regenerating power. While we are unable to see this invisible life-giving source, the affect of His work in us can be seen. Mark 4:41 (AMP): And they were filled with great awe and feared exceedingly and said one to another, Who then is this, that even *wind* and sea obey Him? Subsequently, this means that if the winds are subject to the Lord's voice, He is aware of all that we are facing. He will cause the irregular motion of our atmosphere to shift and accommodate who we are in the spirit. Just as we are unable to see our invisible life source, the pilot of the aircraft cannot see the wind. However, the affects of this tumultuous motion are strongly felt. In this case, your trained pilot makes the necessary adjustments ascending above the chaotic turbulence. Pilots make sure that all the passengers aboard the aircraft are buckled in, where they are secure and safe. If the gusty winds are blowing in your life, remind yourself of this: Your life is in His hands and so are the winds. Ask Him confidently to calm the turbulence. Since God is peace, ask Peace to take a seat next to you until you land safely at your destination.

If the Winds obey Him.....and they do...We should too."

THIS IS LOVE

John 14:21 (NKJV)

He who has My commandments and keeps them, it is he who loves Me. And he who loves Me will be loved by My Father, and I will love him and manifest Myself to him."

The Father in Heaven has given clear cut instructions, "If you love me then keep my commandments." What commandments? The ones He wrote in stone may be a good place to start. When we love someone we should go that extra mile to do what makes them happy. Spending time with the Lord in His Word and in prayer keeps us aware of His will and purpose for our lives. Obeying Him by the grace, He supplies keep us spiritually healthy. Chelsea and Jaylon are always calling me a brat because I love having them in my company. When we share the couch and lounge around together I am able to sharpen their gifts. They quite often sharpen mine as well. They are now at the age where I require a little more obedience. It's like doing their chores on Friday's after school, and curfews respected. Chelsea is 19 and driving. Her original curfew was 1:00 am. I think she now understands the statement I have taken from Saul found in 1 Samuel 15:22 "Obedience is better than Sacrifice." On a few occasions she missed the mark and each time she did the curfew time changed. It is now 11:00 pm. There are blessings that follow the obedient life of a believer. 2 John 1:6 says, This is love that we walk according to His commandments. This is the commandment, that as you have heard from the beginning, you should walk in it. God's instructions are timeless and essential. Love and Obedience are prerequisites as His child. I spend time with the One that can sharpen, strengthen, and correct my ways when I miss my curfew.

This is Love:

"Love one another & Obey my commands"

WE ARE HEALED

Isaiah 53:5 (KJV)

But, He was wounded for our transgressions, He was bruised for our iniquities;
The chastisement for our peace was upon Him, and by His stripes we are healed.

Healed:

1. To make healthy, whole, or sound; restore to health; free from ailment.
2. To bring to an end or conclusion, as conflicts between people or groups, usually with the strong implication of restoring former amity; settle; reconcile.
3. To free from evil; cleanse; purify.

To heal the soul.
How often do you step back and ponder the cross, along with all of its eternal benefits? According to the book of Deuteronomy 25:3 a prisoner could only receive 40 lashes when being beaten as part of the punishment. "Forty blows he may give him and no more, lest he should exceed this and beat him with many blows above these. And your brother is humiliated in your sight." According to Jewish tradition, beating your fellow brother beyond this was public humiliation. JESUS CHRIST, I believe for the purposes of our salvation, endured more than 40 blows that day on Golgotha Hill. His punishers' intentions were to publicly humiliate this King, our Savior, our Lord with the scourging. Consider for a moment, the many ailments we have, for all of them the healing is found in every stripe He took. So I conclude with, Isaiah 53:4-5 (AMP). Surely He has borne our griefs (sicknesses, weaknesses, and distresses) and carried our sorrows and pains [of punishment]. Yet, we [ignorantly] considered Him stricken, smitten, and afflicted by God [as if with leprosy]. But He was wounded for our transgressions; He was bruised for our guilt and iniquities. The chastisement [needful to obtain]

peace and well-being for us was upon Him. And with the stripes [that wounded] Him, we are healed and made whole.

"Each lash restored our life, back to God's original plan, Healthy."

HOLY GHOST BUILT

Jeremiah 18:4 (KJV)

And the vessel that he made of clay was marred in the hand of the potter: so he made it again another vessel, as seemed good to the potter to make it.

The Six Million Dollar Man is an American television series about Steve Austin, a former astronaut with bionic implants working for the OSI (which was usually referred to as the Office of Scientific Intelligence, The Office of Scientific Investigation or the Office of Strategic Intelligence.) Austin is severely injured in the crash and is "rebuilt" in a title-giving operation that costs at least six million dollars. His right arm, both legs and the left eye are replaced by "bionic" implants that enhance his strength, speed and vision far above human norms. He can run at speeds of 60 miles per hour (100 km/h), and his eye has a 20:1 zoom lens and infrared capabilities. He uses his enhanced abilities to work for the OSI (Office of Scientific Intelligence) as a secret agent (and as a guinea pig for bionics). So refreshing to know that we are not guinea pigs but that the Father in Heaven saw our broken bodies, bruised hearts, corrupted minds and devised a clear cut reconstruction. He did not need machines, metal, or synthetic articles to do what was needed to make us whole again, but He in fact placed apart of Himself within us. The Holy Spirit is thc action breathing part of God, in which we are only made strong and able to endure trials because of this living power we have on the inside of us. (Titus 3:5) He saved us-not by works of righteousness that we had done, but according to His mercy, through the washing of regeneration, and renewal by the Holy Spirit. Isaiah 40:29 He gives strength to the weary, and strengthens the powerless. All things are given to us as we concede to being placed on His wheel of reconstruction. The awesome revelation here is, Steve Austin's right arm was rebuilt for strength, God is our righteous arm, what a power. His eyes now see with zoomed infrared capabilities, what needs to be seen according to Romans 8:25: But if we hope for what is still unseen by us, we wait for it with patience and composure. Oh let's not forget the legs that now run at a speed of 60 miles per hour. Who needs to run at this speed when you have knowledge of Isaiah 40:31. But those who trust in the Lord will renew their strength; they will soar on wings like eagles; they will **run** and not grow weary; they will walk and not faint? Therefore, I believe God has made clear our reconstruction according to 2 Corinthians 5:17 therefore if any person is [ingrafted] in Christ (the Messiah) he is a new creation (a new creature altogether); the old [previous moral and spiritual condition] has passed away. Behold, the fresh and new has come! I'd rather and I pray you'd agree the potter's wheel is where we should desire to be. Bionic is electronic devices and mechanical parts to assist humans in performing difficult, dangerous, or intricate tasks, as by supplementing or duplicating parts of the body. Wow sounds to me like the laboratory was complete with lab rats and scientist attempting to do what only the Holy Spirit can, the impossible! The action breathing part of the Godhead has been freely given to us because of the blood that Christ shed for us, an added benefit, we have been doused with "**Super**-natural" power to survive in a natural world. We were born-again, reconstructed, set-apart to live an overt life not undercover or in incognito for OSI. Which means we are Ordained–Sanctified –Intelligence, Operative-Salvation, Intercessor as Operation Salvation Imitators.

The miraculous power of the Holy Spirit takes who we are…..and makes us new!

NO COMPARISON

2 Corinthians 10:12 (ESV)

Not that we dare to classify or compare ourselves with some of those who are commending themselves. But when they measure themselves by one another and compare themselves with one another, they are without understanding.

Be careful not to be unwise, therefore trying to be someone or something that you were not created. There are several reasons, but for the sake of this writing lets just consider first that it must be offensive to the Father. Since, we are certain through His very Word that He devised a plan according to Jeremiah 29:11. His plans are always for good. However, they can be forfeited if we choose not to pick up the mantle. Secondly, your mantle has to be strategically completed by you and you alone. Those who are a part of your task could miss the glory line because you were busy trying to be someone you were not created to be. Or, you could be distracted walking in an assignment that you saw another do. For a fleeting moment, you thought that what they were doing could be your same calling! Oops, you missed your *cue*! Therefore, look at the 3rd reason why comparisons are dangerous. You are not fulfilling your predestined purpose. Your life will not be satisfied. You will forever be searching to fill the empty void that can only be satisfied with GOD'S original architectural plan.

Haggai says it this way:
Now, therefore, thus says the LORD of hosts: Consider your ways. You have sown much, and harvested little. You eat, but you never have enough; you drink, but you never have your fill. You clothe yourselves, but no one is warm. And he who earns wages does so to put them into a bag with holes.

"Without the Master's complete vision, your life story can only be a FABLE"

NOT ASHAMED

Luke 9:26 (NKJV)

For whoever is ashamed of Me and My words, of him the Son of Man will be ashamed when He comes in His own glory, and in His Father's, and of the holy angels.

What an honor to be a voice in the earth to tell others about a risen Savior! I remember as a child growing up Catholic. This meant going to Mass everyday and I do mean everyday. As I got older, I did not want to tell all my friends that my life consisted of church all the time. I knew they were outside on nice summer mornings doing summer things. Today, with great boldness, I declare to all that have an ear to hear that I am in the family of God, and that Jesus Christ is Lord of my soul! Like the writer Paul says, "For I am not ashamed of the gospel of Christ: for it is the power of God unto salvation to everyone that believeth; to the Jew first, and also to the Greek." So I am not ashamed. Excited for every opportunity I get to scribe some newfound revelation for others to read. The simple fact that I have this connection with God the Father, blesses my heart. I want others to experience Him for themselves. However, if I keep it to myself or if you do not open your mouth to tell others of this good news, how else will they know? God does not need us, He is God. He needs nothing: the scripture clearly tell us that our purpose in the earth is to make His name Glorious. He created us to give Him praise. God chose us to be His mouthpiece in this fallen world, where souls are dying for the lack of knowledge of Him. (Hosea 4:6) To be ashamed means to be regretful, or remorseful, even apologetic. What do we have to be ashamed about a loving Savior, or remorseful about? He paid the ransom for us that we ourselves could have never paid on our own. We should boast about His mercy and goodness that will follow us all our days. I am not ashamed that the God I serve has a kingdom that shall never end. (Luke 1:33) Amen!

"Jesus Christ is Lord."

FELT IMPOSSIBLE

Matthew 19:26 (KJV)

But Jesus beheld them, and said unto them, With men this is impossible; but with God all things are possible.

Utilize the resources of your memory bank. Are you tapped in? Would you agree that there have been situations that you believed for certain were impossible to conquer? However, once the gale passed you were able to glance over your shoulder and announce, "I thought I would never get out. It felt impossible." The disciples were astonished at Jesus' words. He spoke in a parable regarding the rich getting into heaven. It was believed that if anyone could make it to heaven it would be the wealthy. Their culture considered the rich especially blessed by God. Jesus crushed this fallacy: He shared how this could actually be a hindrance. What seemingly impossible hurdles are you currently stumbling over each time you raise your feet to finish your course? Be encouraged by this truth: you are equipped with all you need to overcome this grueling obstacle. All you need to do is this, set aside your hindrances and believe that God the Father has already supplied you with all that you need to defeat what appears to be impossible. Jesus said to him, "If you can believe, ALL things *are* possible to him who believes." Human achievement cannot attain salvation, only God has the power to grant it. In the same manner, our difficulties become possible to overcome if we first believe. Then God alone favors us with the grace needed, until we are able to make it completely over our hurdles.

"Do all things through Christ, for He makes the impossible, Possible."

THE AU NATUREL SCAMPER

Mark 14:51-52 (NKJV)

Now a certain young man followed Him, having a linen cloth thrown around his naked body. And the young men laid hold of him, and he left the linen cloth and fled from them naked.

The honest friend warned that they would all commit unthinkable acts though each one was certain He was wrong. However, on the day the accusers came to seize our Lord, His words rang true. Still, His compassion took a front row seat as He watched each of the disciples scurry off to their own spineless ebbs (retreats). Matthew 26:31 & 35: Then saith Jesus unto them, All ye shall be offended because of me this night: for it is written, I will smite the shepherd, and the sheep of the flock shall be scattered abroad. Peter declared, "Even if I have to die with you, I will never disown you." All the other disciples said the same. The Gospel of Mark is the only book that records this event. When you look closely you learn that Mark was not a disciple. Nevertheless, he was curious about all events concerning Jesus. He jots them all down in chronological order in his personal journal. Today, his journal is known as one of the four Gospels. Could it be that the young man that fled naked was in fact Mark? Did he act just like the rest of Christ's followers and scatter for fear that he, too, may be arrested like our compassionate Savior? The disciples along with Christ were having dinner at Mark's house. He was in the bed sleeping when he heard Jesus say they were coming for Him. Mark scurried from his slumber, and all he could find in such a hurry was the sheet that covered his naked body. Researching this portion of scripture, here is another writer's opinion on the subject. It reads; When Jesus said, "**I AM,**" the power that was released was so tremendous that it knocked the soldiers backward. Therefore, evidently it also caused a rumbling in the local cemetery! When that blast of power was released, a young boy, draped in a linen burial cloth in accordance with the tradition of that time, crawled out from his tomb – raised from the dead! The reason he "followed" Jesus was to get a glimpse of the One who had resurrected him. In reading this scripture, I am subject to believe the latter, simply for the purpose of how detailed Mark was when jotting down his experience with Jesus. Why would this differ now? Why would Mark not express that he saw a dead man raised? Why would the other three Gospels not write this same story? After all, the majority of the Gospels are similar. John was the only disciple at the crucifixion, which proved, why Jesus identified him as his beloved. Jesus as God knew that John would be the only one not to flee with the rest. Jesus, so humbly expressed that even though you scatter out of fear, when you witness this coming to pass I will see each of you again in Galilee. Then appoint you to minister and teach everyone to observe all things I have commanded.

"The Au Naturel Scamper was not a disciple
he was a sequential writer."

THE LAST 1ST

Matthew 19:30 (TNIV)

But many who are first will be last,
and many who are last will be first.

Jesus really wants us to get it. He is explaining to the disciples that for all that you were willing to let go of for the cause of following me, you will end up in first place. You may think you are in last place or lagging behind, but it's not true. Many adults are just big kids with more expensive toys. Just look at how we respond to most cases when we don't get our way, "the unsaved appear to have it so much better than us." They have bigger houses, bigger cars, and who holds them accountable? They appear to get away with every manner of mischief. Jesus being God and knowing all things makes it plain. Well He tries, until big mouth Peter proves my point when he says "What about us, what do we have left?" Jesus just wants them to understand that all things the wealthy have obtained, they believe they achieved on their own. Unfortunately, there is a great lack of humility forgetting that their talents and gifts were formed before the world. Gifts, and callings come without repentance (Romans 11:29). The revelation to scribble, Do not forfeit eternal rewards, for temporary benefits, we must be willing to make the sacrifice now for our greater rewards later. Our hearts must be open to accept that while the world does not approve of our being in last place. God already has your 1st Prize ribbon for coming up from behind in the last stretch, which ultimately put you first.

Heavenly Mathematics

"<First_ last > Last + First + lifetime investment = greatness in the kingdom of God."

PROPHETIC FOUNDATION

John 19:31-33 (NKJV)

Therefore, because it was the Preparation Day, that the bodies should not remain on the cross on the Sabbath (for that Sabbath was a high day), the Jews asked Pilate that their legs might be broken, and that they might be taken away. Then the soldiers came and broke the legs of the first and of the other who was crucified with Him. But when they came to Jesus and saw that He was already dead, they did not break His legs.

For these things were done that the Scripture should be fulfilled, "Not one of His bones shall be broken." Psalm 34:20 (NKJV). In the midst of pandemonium, the Roman soldiers were trying to keep the law, so they could eat the Passover meal. It was customary for the Roman soldiers to break the victims' legs to hasten the death process. In this way, they could remove the bodies from the cross. When a person hung on a cross, death came by suffocation. The victims would use their legs to hold themselves up and push using the strength of their legs against the cross to keep breathing. With broken legs, he would suffocate almost immediately. Christ is our Passover Lamb, the perfect sacrifice for our sin. This voluntary death of Jesus before His legs could be broken was in fulfillment of **Psalm 34:19 (MSG)** Disciples often get into trouble, still, GOD is there every time. He is your bodyguard, shielding every bone; not even a finger gets broken. Not breaking the bones of the lamb foreshadowed Jesus' death: None of the Savior's bones were broken. The Passover Lamb was to be without blemish, which meant also that, although Jesus was to be slain on the cross, none of His bones could be broken. This prophetic word written in the Old Testament was intended for believers to know that it was speaking of the coming Lamb of God, whose bones were providentially kept from being broken. God's plans are favorable in justice and righteous; legs are a core part of our foundation. They could crucify Christ. However, they could not destroy

His foundation. For His foundation is found in glory with His Father. There is no one that will ever be able to destroy the Creator's foundation. Another requirement was that the lamb was not to be left until the morning. **Numbers 9:12 (KJV):** They shall leave none of it unto the morning, nor break any bone of it: according to all the ordinances of the Passover, they shall keep it. Jesus did not hang on the cross for several days. This was not a coincidence. There are no coincidences with God only planned purposes. Had He done so, He could not be our Passover. He was sacrificed on the day before a Sabbath for a reason. His executioners, either Jewish or Roman, did not suspect that they were doing God's will by crucifying Him that day.

"Without the Passover Lamb
we would be doomed to spiritual death."

EPISODE FIVE

A PLETHORA OF GRACE

Matthew 16:18 (NKJV)

And I also say to you that you are Peter, and on this rock I will build My church, and the gates of Hades shall not prevail against it.

THE 12 HE CHOSE

WOMEN TOO

NOTHING BOGUS

SO MANY QUESTIONS

MERCI THOMAS

CHOSEN DISCIPLES

COMPASSIONATE HEART

THE TAX COLLECTOR

ENTHUSIASTIC JAMES

JOHN HIS BELOVED

PETER PETROS

THE 12 HE CHOSE

Luke 6:13 (NLT)

At daybreak, he called together all of his disciples and chose twelve of them to be apostles.

Here are their names:

Simon Peter - was impulsive. Later, was bold when speaking about Jesus Christ.

Andrew - was eager to witness to others about Christ.

James – was ambitious, short-tempered, judgmental, but deeply committed to Jesus.

John – was ambitious and judgmental, but later was very loving.

Phillip - had a questioning attitude.

Bartholomew (Nathanael) – was honest and straightforward.

Thomas – had courage and doubted.

Matthew (Levi) - despised outcast because of his dishonest career as a tax collector.

James - preached until his death.

Thaddeus – was warm-hearted.

Simon – had fierce patriotism.

Judas Iscariot - was treacherous, greedy, and ultimately betrayed Jesus.

Matthias - replaced Judas.

"Jesus called them, and He called you, too."

WOMEN TOO

Luke 8:1-3 (MSG)

He continued according to plan, traveled to town after town, village after village, preaching God's kingdom, spreading the Message. The Twelve were with him. There were also some women in their company who had been healed of various evil afflictions and illnesses: Mary, the one called Magdalene, from whom seven demons had gone out; Joanna, wife of Chuza, Herod's manager; and Susanna—along with many others who used their considerable means to provide for the company.

In First Century Jewish culture, women were almost insignificant and in most cases, they were treated like a second-class citizens with very little rights. Nevertheless, thank God for His loving Son Jesus who for the sake of love and equality crossed those barriers. Jesus possessed with a special sensitivity that, as we peer closer, we will realize only a Savior can. Jesus had done some amazing exploits in the lives of these women. He cast out demons, others He healed, He fed them, He taught them, but in the end of it, they all knew He really loved them.

These are they:

Jesus speaks to the Samaritan woman at the well.

Jesus raises a widow's son from the dead.

A sinful woman anoints Jesus' feet.

Jesus forgives the adulterous woman.

Jesus visits Mary and Martha.

Jesus healed the crippled women.

Jesus heals the daughter of a Gentile woman.

Weeping women follow Jesus to the cross.

Jesus' mother Mary and other women gather at the cross.

Jesus appears to Mary Magdalene.

Jesus appears to women first after His resurrection.

"Jesus' pays a ransom for the sinner Theresa Kirk."

NOTHING BOGUS

~Bartholomew~

John 1:45-51 (GW)

Philip found Nathanael and told him, "We have found the man whom Moses wrote about in his teachings and whom the prophets wrote about. He is Jesus, son of Joseph, from the city of Nazareth." Nathanael said to Philip, "Can anything good come from Nazareth? Philip told him, "Come and see!" Jesus saw Nathanael coming toward him and remarked, "Here is a true Israelite who is sincere." Nathanael asked Jesus, "How do you know anything about me? Jesus answered him, "I saw you under the fig tree before Philip called you." Nathanael said to Jesus, "Rabbi, you are the Son of God! You are the king of Israel!"

If Jesus was standing in the same room with you, would you know Him? Apparently, Nathanael "aka" Bartholomew knew the moment he fixed his eyes on Him. What did Bartholomew mean in his response to Phillip "Can anything good come from Nazareth?" Perhaps, Bartholomew remembered the words spoken about this Kings birth. Whereby stating this; Jesus would be born in Bethlehem, not Nazareth, Bartholomew must have been aware of this fact because his conviction was clear until he saw Jesus' face. Then straight from his heart riddled by his lips; "Rabbi, you are the Son God! You are the king of Israel!" His curiosity caused him to go and get a glimpse of the one the Prophets had written about in the Scriptures. If Bartholomew had kept his own prejudice, without investigating this rumor, he would have missed the Messiah. Unlike Phillip, asking Jesus to reveal the Father, Bartholomew knew, tout de suite that he was standing in the presence of greatness. Jesus was polished with glory goodness, doused with loving-kindness, and full of grace. Yes, Jesus was correct when He said, "Here is a true Israelite who is sincere." The Israelite declared, "God has chosen." Candidly stating; "There is nothing **BOGUS** about this one, nothing at all."

"Nothing Bogus about God's elect, & yes that means you."

SO MANY QUESTIONS

~Philip~

John 14:7-9 (NKJV)

"If you had known Me, you would have known My Father also; and from now on you know Him and have seen Him."

Philip said to Him, "Lord, show us the Father, and it is sufficient for us."

Jesus said to him, "Have I been with you so long and yet you have not known Me, Philip? He who has seen Me has seen the Father; so how can you say, 'Show us the Father?

Oops, another one bites the dust! Philip put his foot in his mouth. Jesus came to reveal the Father. He had just told His 12 comrades, "If you had known Me, you would have known My Father also; and from now on you know Him and have seen Him." However, like Thomas, Philip must have been slow to comprehend. Jesus rebuked him because Philip should have known the answer to his own question. Philip, along with Andrew, approached Jesus saying that the Greeks wanted to see Him. (John 12:20) In their lack of understanding, this illustration again proved that Jesus wanted to make the apostles aware that His purpose was clear. He was born to die for all of them that would believe. I guess we should cut Philip some slack. Maybe, he was just the kind of guy that liked dealing with the hard-nosed facts.

"God uses our questions to teach us, ask and it will be given to you."

MERCI THOMAS

John 20:24-29 (NKJV)

Now Thomas, called the Twin, one of the twelve, was not with them when Jesus came. The other disciples therefore said to him, "We have seen the Lord."
So he said to them, "Unless I see in His hands the print of the nails, and put my finger into the print of the nails, and put my hand into His side, I will not believe."
And after eight days His disciples were again inside, and Thomas with them. Jesus came, the doors being shut, and stood in the midst, and said, "Peace to you!" Then He said to Thomas, "Reach your finger here, and look at My hands; and reach your hand here, and put it into My side. Do not be unbelieving, but believing." And Thomas answered and said to Him, "My Lord and my God!" Jesus said to him, Thomas, because you have seen Me, you have believed. Blessed are those who have not seen "and yet have believed."

Notice the doors were locked. How did He get inside? Jesus' new resurrected body was no longer subject to natural laws or locked doors as it was prior to His death. He was not a ghost or an apparition. Jesus could be touched and was able to eat. In awestruck wonder, Thomas was standing face-to-face with His resurrected Lord! Thomas was able to do just as he desired, touch and see the Saviors nail scarred hands, then put his own hand into Jesus' side. Once this confirmation took place, Thomas believed, calling Him "My Lord My God." This authentic communion between a Savior and His friend was not just for Thomas' faith but for ours too. "Thomas, because you have seen Me, you have believed. Blessed are those who have not seen, 'and yet have believed." Without question, our doubtful Tommy's reservations inspired Jesus to pronounce this eternal blessing. Merci, Thomas! Obviously, Jesus does not reject doubts that are honest, and directed toward belief. When we find ourselves in a doubting state of mind, we should take this life lesson from Thomas: Admit that it exists then allow God to turn that disbelief into belief. Silent doubts rarely find answers; doubt was not intended to be a permanent condition in the life of a believer.

"Doubt encourages re-thinking."

CHOSEN DISCIPLES

Luke 6:15-16 (KJV)

Matthew and Thomas, James the son of Alphaeus,
and Simon called Zealot,
And Judas the brother of James, and Judas Iscariot,
which also was the traitor.

Called by the Master! Wow! What an honor! Yes, an honor, because He knows all there is to know about us. Yet, He still called and gifted us for the job we have been slated to carry out here on earth. Just look at these three; James-the less, Simon-the Zealot (another way of saying activist, or maniac), and then you have Judas-the traitor. When Jesus chose His disciples, He was not looking for front page models or perfect men to do the job. He was looking for real people. Jesus chose people that would be changed by His love. He sent them out to communicate that salvation was available to everyone. Jesus especially wanted to reach those whose lives were marked by failure. We may wonder what Jesus sees in us when He calls us to be His disciples. We must believe that Jesus accepts us. In spite of our humanity, He can use ordinary people just like you and me to achieve His extraordinary work. Understand that discipleship, from salvation to glorification, is by God's grace through faith. The calling of Jesus is gracious and inviting; adventurous and unsettling. However, it is a choice, originating with God and fulfilled in simple obedience. Like these disciples, we are not called to be modern-day heroes. We are just simply called to pick up our cross and follow Him. When we have come through, we are to tell others that they, too, have been chosen.

"There was no casting call, you were simply Chosen
to be His Disciple."

COMPASSIONATE HEART

John 1:40-41 (HCSB)

Andrew, Simon Peter's brother, was one of the two who heard John and followed Him. He first found his own brother Simon and told him, "We have found the Messiah!" (which means "Anointed One")

Andrew, Peter's little brother had a big heart, and was known to be a man of few words. He was truly the opposite of his big mouth brother. Andrew's name means: having qualities traditionally ascribed to men of strength, bravery and manly character. It was Andrew that eagerly introduced Peter to Christ. Since they were brothers, he had to have known of Peter's domineering attitude, which would make Peter the boss. However, Andrew still for the purposes of the Kingdom brought Peter to Jesus anyway. Andrew was a man driven with a passion for the truth. Therefore, when he and John heard John the Baptist's declaration of the Messiah, they quickly left him and went to follow Christ. Excitement coupled with Messianic thrill, is what made Andrew bold, deliberate, and decisive when telling others about the Lamb of God. Almost everything scripture tells us about Andrew allows us to see he had a great heart and desired to be effective in ministry. Andrew never demanded to be in the limelight; he simply wanted to serve and tell others about Jesus. Notice the first thing Andrew did once he was certain he had met the Messiah. He went straight to the one person in the world he loved and brought him to Christ. This life-changing experience was too good to keep to himself. Kingdom-builders have immense hearts. They, like Andrew, once in the presence of Christ, seek to see and believe the impossible can be made possible. It was Andrew that took the boy with 5 loaves of bread, and 2 fish to Christ. Perhaps because he witnessed Christ change Peter's life, Andrew knew Christ would change the lives of all of those that witnessed this feeding miracle too. Andrew was compassionate regarding his assignment to show & tell others about the Messiah.

Matthew 5:8 (KJV)

"Blessed are *the pure in heart for they shall see God."*

THE TAX COLLECTOR

Matthew 9:9-13 (ESV)

As Jesus passed on from there, he saw a man called Matthew sitting at the tax booth, and He said to him, "Follow me." And he rose and followed Him.

When was the last time you considered having an IRS agent over for dinner? Matthew 9:10, And as Jesus reclined at a table in the house, behold, many tax collectors and "sinners" came and were reclining with Jesus and his disciples. Matthew 9:11-12, And when the Pharisees saw this, they said to His disciples, 'Why does your teacher eat with tax collectors and sinners?' But, when he heard it, he said, 'Those who are well have no need of a physician, but those who are sick. Go and learn what this means. I desire mercy, and not sacrifice. For I came not to call the righteous, but sinners." Talk about the pot calling the kettle black, were the Pharisees delusional that they too were in the same category as those that they were pointing their fingers? Talk about hypocritical. I believe Matthew knew the only way for these fellow partners-in-crime to be saved would be to introduce them to his new-found Savior. Because of his line of work, Matthew was not allowed in any of the churches. However, look closely at Matthew's Gospel; he often quoted Old Testament scriptures. Could it be that Matthew's spiritual hunger caused him to leave all that he had to follow Jesus? There is something powerful and transforming about the revelation of God. Once you are aware of Him, you drop your own agendas, and then follow Him to the cross. After all, who wants to be a social outcast or a hoodlum despised by many, and regarded as a lowlife? In Christ, Matthew found a friend that introduced him to a new way of living, he was no longer rejected. Matthew's gnawing hunger for deliverance was stronger than the hypocritical and thieving habitual lifestyle he previously knew. Jesus said to them, "Truly, I say to you, the tax collectors and the prostitutes go into the kingdom of God before you." (Matthew 21:31). So I conclude that everything God does has perfect purpose. He called Matthew, and Matthew brought to Christ: all of them that were just like him. So it goes with us, He called you on purpose. How many will you bring to Him?

"Not rejected, but accepted."

ENTHUSIASTIC JAMES

Matthew 4:21 (NKJV)

Going on from there, He saw two other brothers, James the son of Zebedee, and John his brother, in the boat with Zebedee their father, mending their nets. He called them.

James had a fiery temperament; he was outspoken, exaggerated, and impatient with evildoers. In his day and age, I guess it would be safe to say that James was a modern-day enthusiast for JC Ministries. Zeal is an asset, but only when truly used for righteousness' sake. Apart from this, it is simply destructive behavior. James & John were not called, "The Sons of Thunder," for nothing. Their quick tongues, along with clinched fists and "put 'em up" attitudes, kept them in timeouts. Jesus' rejection by a Samaritan village on His way to Jerusalem made these thunder boys quite miffed. This annoyed pair inquired of Jesus saying, "Lord, do You want us to command fire to come down from heaven and consume them, just as Elijah did?" But He turned and rebuked them saying, "You do not know what manner of spirit you are of. For the Son of Man did not come to destroy men's lives but to save *them.*" And they went to another village. Arrogance gets you no place in glory, especially where Christ is concerned. Please believe He is concerned for everyone, even the Samaritans. Unlike Elijah who used his zeal to show-off our grand God, the brothers wanted to exploit their talented swagger. They thought the stage belonged to them. James and John wanted to float their own boat. There was another incident where they lobbied help from their Mother to assist them in getting a high seat in the kingdom. The revelation is this, every part of who we are good, bad, and indifferent, God will use for His great good. Passion such as this which James displayed once molded by the Holy Spirit, is powerfully effective in the kingdom God!

"Surrender the thunder in you to God."

JOHN HIS BELOVED

John 13:23 (NKJV)

Now there was leaning on Jesus' bosom one of His disciples, whom Jesus loved.

Another Thunder boy converted. John was not a soft, easy-going, cannot wait to hang-out-with kind of man. Not in the least. John, much like his older brother James, exhibited the same zealous ambition, intolerance, and sometimes explosive nature. However, John was nicknamed "the Apostle of Love." He wrote in the New Testament more on the topic of Love than any other biblical author. He scribed the importance of our ability of loving one another and Christ's love for the church, and its members. John's passion for the truth shaped the way he wrote; clear in black-and-white: not much gray area in his letters to the church. John, I would say is antithetical. While he agrees that sin is sin and should not be a practice for the believer, he does not belabor this point. Instead, John focuses on how we as believers should try most earnestly to live a life in love and peace. The Apostle of Love always wrote in a warm, soothing pattern that reflected his deep convictions, along with his absolute devotion to the truth. Like many of us, in his younger days, John seemed to have a lack of spiritual equilibrium. There is a balance needed in order to identify the complete purpose and attributes of our character to benefit us properly for kingdom good. If we are not careful, our best characteristic could be our greatest pitfall. We can swiftly become corrupted by our own sin, which causes us to stumble. Our human depravity directs each of us down this beaten-path. Even as a writer, I am still uncertain regarding many things. Yet, I proclaim this one thing I am confident of, I am glad that the Christ extremist took time to journal the important aspects of change which enable the believer to live a life of *Love* because God is *Love*. Thanks John, for the thunderous attitude!

"Without LOVE there is no thunder."

PETER PETROS

Matthew 16:16-18 (KJV)

Simon Peter answered and said, Thou art the Christ, the Son of the living God. And Jesus answered and said unto him, Blessed art thou, Simon Bar-jonah: for flesh and blood hath not revealed it unto thee, but my Father which is in heaven. And I say also unto thee, That thou art Peter, and upon this rock I will build my church; and the gates of hell shall not prevail against it.

Petra denotes "a mass of rock," as distinct from Petros, "a detached stone or boulder," or a stone that might be thrown or easily moved. (Greek)

Jesus is really calling you the Rock? Jaw drops to the floor, mouth is wide open, and for a moment you think, "S-e-r-i-o-u-s-l-y? Me?" Me, the one that will deny you three times that dreadful day on Calvary? Who me, the big mouth, quick-to-fight Peter? Maybe, that is why you will use me. My tenacity, coupled with my fighter instincts, is what will be needed for the greater works. Calling Peter a rock, when Peter was more like Jell-O was deliberate. Peter must have known he could not live up to his new identity on his own. He needed help. It is the same for us - we cannot live the Christian life in our own might. It calls us to be people we cannot be in our strength. Just like Peter, we need help from the true Rock. We need His grace to live. Psalm 18:2 (NKJV), "The LORD is my rock and my fortress and my deliverer; My God, my strength, in whom I will trust; my shield and the horn of my salvation, my stronghold." Christ is the solid Rock, *(Petra);* however, it was Peter's confession here that Jesus edicts him as (*Petros-stone/solid*). Whenever Christ referred to Peter as Simon, it was a subtle message to remind him of his old man. However, when he called him "Rock" or Peter, He was affirming his true authority. With this understanding, it is no wonder Jesus tells Peter (Petros) that Satan desired to sift him as wheat. At every angle, that sly devil was trying to destroy the church before it could reach the lost. Jesus assured Peter that he would not fail in his faith because the One who called him would be praying for him. Have you ever considered that is the only reason why your faith has not gone kaput? I suggest that the One who called you for purpose is praying that your faith will not fail. However, what is even greater is that Christ knew who Simon Peter would turn out to be. He called him by that name, "ROCK." Once again, confirming that when God called us, He did it knowing that in the end He would perfect who He called us to be. Theresa means "reaper and one who harvests." I plan to reap the harvest He designed with my life in mind. Kirk means "church," well you get the picture. What's in your name? I bet it has destiny written all over it.

"Because we are Petros,
Petra will continue to pray."

EPISODE SIX

WHAT IF HE

Proverbs 11:30 (NKJV)

The fruit of the righteous is a tree of life; and he that winneth souls is wise.

IDENTITY CRISIS

Matthew 4:7-11 (NKJV)

Jesus said to him, "It is written again, 'You shall not tempt the LORD your God.'
Again, the devil took Him up on an exceedingly high mountain, and showed Him all the kingdoms of the world and their glory.
And he said to Him, "All these things I will give You if You will fall down and worship me." Then Jesus said to him, "Away with you, Satan! For it is written, 'You shall worship the LORD your God, and Him only you shall serve."
Then the devil left Him, and behold, angels came and ministered to Him.

God never tempts us to sin, that is Satan's specialty. Satan surely forgot that Jesus was God. Jesus knew that Satan was trying to manipulate Him by asking for a sign. We know that the enemy knows the Word. Therefore, he tried to convince Jesus to sin by using the Word Jesus as God wrote…..Not very clever devil. The issue was not the temptation, but the motive behind it. The enemy often appeals to our pride, rather than us trusting God, the enemy hopes we will take matters into our own hands. For Jesus, turning the stones to bread would have not been trusting, His Father. This test came for Jesus to accomplish God's will: He had to face the devil and prevail. Paul tells us in the book of Ephesians that in order for us to overcome the scandalous plots set by a crafty enemy we must, "Put on the whole armor of God." In this way, we may be able to stand against the wiles (schemes) of the devil. God cannot be tempted by evil, so why the test? God had to show the world and the devil that Christ was tempted, yet He never sinned. For a moment, Satan must have forgotten that Jesus was God. Satan's selfish pride got him evicted from heaven. He was still trying in his crafty little way, to receive worship that is reserved for God alone. Again, not a clever devil. While

Satan definitely had the right to offer Christ the world, he was trying to distort Jesus' perspective by making Him focus on worldly power and not on God's original plan. Although Satan may possibly have forgotten that Jesus was God, Jesus had no identity crisis. Jesus knows who He is, and to whom He belongs. He knew the purpose of the test, and said to the devil, "It is also written, 'You must not tempt the Lord your God.' " Oh, yeah. By the way, Satan did not lead Jesus to the temptation: the Holy Spirit did, just as it goes with us. Spiritual victories are often followed by tests. The spirit lead Jesus into the wilderness to try His faith, but the wicked one tried to seduce Jesus, just as he does with us. Satan flashes worldly fame and entice us with material things which only last for a fleeting moment. I prefer Jesus on any day; for the peace that surpasses all understanding, and mercy promised daily.

"Temptation does not have to end in failure.
Look at Jesus when tempted."

GOD WITH US

Matthew 1:21-23 (NKJV)

"And she will bring forth a Son, and you shall call His name JESUS, for He will save His people from their sins." So all this was done that it might be fulfilled which was spoken by the Lord through the prophet, saying: "Behold, the virgin shall be with child, and bear a Son, and they shall call His name Immanuel, which is translated, "God with us."

From His birth, Jesus Christ was unblemished, and born of the pure Virgin Mary. He was begotten of the Holy Ghost, without a taint of sin. Jesus' soul was pure and spotless as the driven snow, white, clear and perfect. His life was the same. In Him was no sin. He took our infirmities and bore our sorrows on the cross. He was in all points tempted as we are, but there was that sweet exception, "without sin." Christ, the lamb without blemish. You who have known the Lord, who has tasted of his grace, and who has experienced fellowship with him, does not your heart acknowledge that He is the Lamb without spot or blemish? Can you find any fault with your Savior? Have you anything to lay to His charge? Has His faithfulness ceased? Have His words been defective or broken? Has His promises deteriorated? Has He forgotten His engagements or contract concerning you? In addition, in can you find any error in Him? Ah, no! He is the unblemished Lamb! Jesus is the pure, spotless, Immaculate, *"Lamb of God who takes away the sin of the world."* In Him, there is no sin. Yes, this lamb is God with us!

"The spotless, unblemished Lamb, saved my life."

THE DOCTOR'S IN

Colossians 4:14 (KJV)

Luke, the beloved physician, and Demas, greet you.

Paul's road-dog, his buddy, ole' pal was a smart guy. Luke was a Greek, Gentile Christian, a doctor as well as, a man of science and detail. Oh, and for the record, Mr. Smarty Pants is also the writer of the book of Acts. Dr. Luke in his interpretation of the precious life of Jesus Christ scribes as if he were the attending physician at our Savior's birth. Let us not forget he was also the au natural scamper at the time they came to seize Jesus for the cross. Luke's occupation explains even further, as to why he was a man of great detailed. Think about it. When you go for your annual physical, do you want your Doctor leaving any important details out of your diagnosis? It is because of Luke we are able to get a closer look at the comprehensive accounts of our compassionate Lord's life. I imagine Luke's approach when he sat down to scribe the book of Acts. You remember the book that makes clear our sole purpose to walking our Christian journey? Acts is the book that records the church's birthday. Consider a sequel to his Gospel found in the New Testament known as the "Book of Luke." This author gives the most specific accounts about our Savior. Of his writing on Jesus, the Doctor (author) offers: His birth, childhood, and the development of His ministry. Luke's approach was to ensure we see the humanity in Jesus as our Savior. He was fully prepared to live a perfect life. For instance, Luke's personal and thorough perspective included stories that demonstrate Jesus' interest in the non-Jewish world, women, and the poor.

"I thank God for the Doctor's brass account of my Savior's life."

THEY CHOSE THE SEDITIONIST

Mark 15:6-7 (NKJV)

Now at the feast he was accustomed to releasing one prisoner to them, whomever they requested. And there was one named Barabbas, who was chained with his fellow rebels; they had committed murder in the rebellion.

Seriously, they put a seditionist back out on the unpaved streets of Jerusalem? Barabbas, obviously a liar, was also a cheating scoundrel. As if those crimes were not enough, he was also a murderer. Talk about an unfair trial. Since Barabbas was a known rebel, maybe Pilate thought the screaming, angry crowd would come to their senses and release the King and not this iniquitous villain. Do you wonder if this shady Barabbas felt any guilt? Was he conjuring up his next heinous rebellion? Did he stand around gawking at this King on the cross? Did he barrel out of the courts, thinking they may change their minds? Pilate knew that Jesus was innocent. However, he disregarded his heart, even after his wife's dream. Pilate succumbed to be a crowd-pleaser. Just like us: we do not listen to our hearts or the Lord's voice. Instead, we rationalize with what says the crowd. What a commentary on human nature! A day in the life of Christ; rejected by His disciples, condemned by the Roman council, and denied by Peter three times. Then, He must take the place of a seditionist. The reality on this matter is we too once rejected Him, before we knew Him we condemned Him. At one point, we denied Him. However, Jesus looked past the cross, and was completely obedient to His Father's divine will. He not only took the place of the Seditionist, He also took our place that dreadful day on Golgotha Hill.

"Choose wisely, choose Christ."

HE CHOSE YOU

Mark 1:17 (MSG)

Jesus said to them, "Come with me. I'll make a new kind of fisherman out of you. I'll show you how to catch men and women instead of perch and bass."

Sit back. Think for a moment about the crew Jesus chose as His posse. They were judgmental, short-tempered, greedy, militant, doubtful, and despised by many. Yet, they were chosen to walk with the King. Jesus as God is strategic in all His actions. Would you agree? Like many of us, Jesus had terms of endearments to address those that were close to Him. These are the names for His Apostles; Peter was the "Rock," James and John were the "Sons of Thunder," Andrew was a "Fisher of Men," and Bartholomew was a "True Israelite." And then there was Judas, "a devil." The interesting thing about this posse is they all had issues. Just like us! However, the Love of Christ transformed these lives for the ultimate greater good, which was for the Kingdom. You were, exclusively favored to walk with the King. In fact, He chose you, too. This snippet should cause you to dance with joy to know that when Christ sought after you it was simply because He saw who you were in His future. He is the potter: we are the clay. He is molding and perfecting us to have His own way, and we must be willing to walk with Him on our journey. He desires for us to shut out the voices of our past, while adhering to the voice of our designed future. Take this nugget and go far. We are in time, but with God there is no time just eternity. For He is the eternal God. Therefore, when God chose us, He elected us from eternity to live, eternally with Him. However, the only way this is possible is just as it were with the disciples. Believers are transformed by His love from what we used to be to what He has planned for our lives.

"Not perfect, just chosen."

WHO OR WHAT IS MOTIVATING YOU?

Matthew 12:34 (KJV)

O generation of vipers, how can ye, being evil, speak good things? For out of the abundance of the heart the mouth speaketh.

Words are life and the wrong words have the power to kill. God is love, and we should speak to one another in a manner that in our speech we put God on display. Jesus was evidently teaching us how to identify the condition of one's heart. We cannot fix our heart problems. However, if we fix the condition of our speech, we bring glory to God who requires it. The Holy Spirit is there to assist us in our attitudes and its motives. So what or who motivates your speech?

Our speech when motivated by the Holy Spirit in
His infinite wisdom:

Mercy
Love for everyone
Peace all over it
Consideration for others
Submission
Sincerity and impartial
Righteousness
Compassion
Long-suffering
Generosity

Our speech when motivated by Satan the liar/murderer:

Bitterness
Envy

Selfish ambitions
Manipulation
Disorder
Evil
Deceitful
Slanderous
Full of lies
Hate
Contention
Strife

"Love can quickly end a fight, just look at the Cross."

HUMILITY VS. PRIDE

1 Peter 5:6 (NKJV)

Humble yourselves therefore under the mighty hand of God, that he may exalt you in due time:

Humility; the state of being humble; lack of pride.
Pride; an excessive high opinion of self; conceit.

Humility leads to wisdom.
Pride leads to disgrace.

Humility takes advice.
Pride produces quarrels.

Humility leads to life.
Pride leads to punishment & destruction.

Humility ends in honor.
Pride ends in downfall.

Humility brings one to honor.
Pride brings one low.

"Staying humble involves working with His power according to His Guidance."

FIGHTING FAIR

Psalms 144:1 (KJV)

Blessed be the LORD my strength, which teacheth my hands to war, and my fingers to fight:

Ephesians 6:12 (GW)

This is not a wrestling match against a human opponent. We are wrestling with rulers, authorities, the powers who govern this world of darkness, and spiritual forces that control evil in the heavenly world.

Fighting fair? What a ludicrous title. Just keep reading. It will make absolute sense in just a bit. I was kickboxing during a recent workout session with my trainer. While practicing several moves, my trainer told me I was not punching, jabbing, or kicking properly. To make matters worse, she said I also wasn't blocking or guarding myself to prevent getting hurt. My response simply expressed what I believed was precise. "I am not coordinated." Instantaneously, I heard the Holy Spirit say to me, "You don't know how to fight, and you don't fight fair!" Ouch! I knew exactly what He was conveying to me. In a present trial, I took it upon myself not to pray concerning an irritating situation in my life. By not praying, I was not fighting fairly. Rather, I was justifying my actions by holding the person hostage with my distasteful attitude, along with occasional reckless banter. The crazy part about this is that I knew how to change the situation. Nevertheless, I chose to fight naturally, and not spiritually. My decision not to fight fair had completely excluded God's hand as my referee while in the ring. Therefore, because of whom my referee is and what He says about fighting, the legitimate way would have been to pray concerning each step. Then, casting down my own thoughts. We have all been justified by grace. Ultimately, a "fair fighter" only fights their true enemy. In this case, just as noted in the above scripture, we are not to fight one another physically or verbally. But we are to come strongly against the spirit of that, which has waged a war for our life. Fundamentally, the enemy comes to kill, steal, and destroy. If I for once had gotten out of my emotions and stepped in the spirit, I would be effective in warfare against the enemy. I ponder a few vital theories. First, would I have had to go all 12 rounds? Second, if I fought fairly when I heard the initial "ding-ding" could it have been over with a "TKO" in the 1st round? Obviously, I clearly see that when the ref called me to the center for ethical boxing ring rules and regulations, I was not paying attention. If I were, I would have never hit below the belt. Lastly, three judges score each round. Therefore, we need not whine or plead our case. The judges are shrewdly watching every move and blow we take. They have decreed I win!

"Fighting God's way, we are promised a
Win in every Fracas."

GOOD FRUIT

Matthew 7:16-18 (KJV)

Ye shall know them by their fruits. Do men gather grapes of thorns, or figs of thistles? Even so every good tree bringeth forth good fruit; but a corrupt tree bringeth forth evil fruit. A good tree cannot bring forth evil fruit, neither can a corrupt tree bring forth good fruit.

There are pseudo-Christians everywhere! How do we identify them? I think the scripture above makes it clear. If my intentions are to go to my local nursery and pick up an apple tree, then I expect the nursery to sell me an apple tree, not an orange, fig, or plum tree. Unfortunately, there are those in society who purposely take advantage of God's people by how they falsely interpret the Word. Some claim to be scholars of the Word, and yet they are false Prophets ready with their "parking lot prophesies." Why did Jesus admonish us about observing the fruit from the tree? I believe He is teaching us how to quickly identify those pseudo-Christians. Taking the time to inspect and witness the fruit they produce is a clear-cut way for us to examine the lives of such pseudo-Christians. Let's consider the tree again for a moment. If I intended on growing an apple tree but later see oranges, can I trust the nursery where I made my purchase? Should I continue to support their business? In the book of Galatians, Paul describes how good fruit should look, act, and taste. Paul describes the fruit this way; "But the fruit of the Spirit is love, joy, peace, patience, kindness, goodness, faith, gentleness, self-control. Against such things there is no law." Now those who belong to Christ Jesus have crucified the flesh with its passions and desires. Therefore, if one claims to be a nevertheless follower of Christ, you can quickly identify them by such fruitful facts. Being good fruit was not intended be a laborious or flamboyant task. Consider this final example. Some specialty stores sell plastic fruit for displays or props.

In a theatrical play, you will even find a bowl on a nicely decorated table with plastic made to look like edible fruit. But, be wise and study, so you are aware of the phony fruit.

"You can pretend all you want, but who you are I see in your fruit."

GREATEST INTERCESSOR

Romans 8:26-27 (NLV)

In the same way, the Holy Spirit helps us where we are weak. We do not know how to pray or what we should pray for, but the Holy Spirit prays to God for us with sounds that cannot be put into words. God knows the hearts of men. He knows what the Holy Spirit is thinking. The Holy Spirit prays for those who belong to Christ the way God wants Him to pray.

Grateful to be a believer of Christ. Because of Him, we are not left alone to cope with our problems. When we do not always know how to pray according to His will, the Holy Spirit not only prays with you but also for you, and God answers. Hallelujah! God tells us, "His Word has to accomplish that which He sent it out to do." God is praying with us. Since He knows what He has for us, we can rest in the assurance knowing that we have what we requested in prayer. Jude instructs, "Build your lives up in your most holy faith and pray in the Holy Spirit." In the scripture referenced above, Paul paints a great visual here. Imagine you are the child, and your heavenly Father is kneeling and praying alongside of you. Therefore, the next time you take your request to Him, trust and believe He will do what is best for you. God prays with us concerning "all things" – not just isolated incidents. No, not just the tragic things or just the small things. Yes, God prays with us concerning even the fearful things – then He answers for our good.

"Here I am again Father, what shall we pray?"

JESUS WEPT

John 11:35 (KJV)

Jesus wept.

No other Gospel records this event. I wonder why. Perhaps, it is because John, the one who Christ loved so, was there to witness it. Nevertheless, John wanted us to look at this compassionate Savior in His humanness. Martha and Mary were highly-grieved, and had every right, their brother Lazarus had died. However, Jesus asked a very loaded question, "Do you believe?" They replied, "Yes!" They coupled their faith with the power of Christ. The sisters witnessed a miracle as their brother Lazarus, who been dead four days, rose from the dead under Jesus' command. At first glance, it appears that the sisters are upset with Jesus for taking so long to get to them. When Jesus initially became aware that Lazarus was deathly ill, Jesus had a prophetic response. "This sickness is not unto death, but for the glory of God, that the Son of God might be glorified thereby." However, Jesus had a heart for the siblings as well. He too, loved Lazarus. Undoubtedly, He understood their pain and sympathized with them. We should be the same with Christ: do not hide our emotions from Him, after-all He already knows. Therefore, when confess our true matters of the heart it shows Him we believe. The writer of Hebrews proves this fact in chapter 4 verse 15, "For we do not have a High Priest who is unable to sympathize with us." Can you find a reference anywhere in the Bible where it states that Jesus was laughing? No. Because, there is none. Throughout scripture, you will always find all points showing Him as a loving, tenderhearted, caring individual, who wanted nothing more for us than peace. Verse 33 says, "He groaned in the spirit and was troubled." Frustrated is what I believe is depicted here. Possibly, Jesus was disturbed over the fact that He was witnessing disbelief. Jesus spoke to Martha saying, "Thy brother shall rise again." She swiftly replies, "I know in the resurrection at that last day." Jesus takes His plight a little further by explaining, "I am the resurrection." Martha put the correlation together that, "Yes." He is the, "true," life-giver. Remember, Martha and Mary had a house full of mourners. Thus, Jesus' statement in verse 15 makes His intentions very clear. There was a purpose in Him not rushing to get to His friend's bed-side. Jesus' response to what appears to be a lack of urgency, or unemotional reaction was deliberate, and had a powerful commission attached to it. His unadulterated modus operandi was to demonstrate beyond question both His gift of prophecy and omnipotence.

"Believe, so you do not cause your risen Savior to weep."

EPISODE SEVEN

SALT

James 3:12 (AMP)

Can a fig tree, my brethren, bear olives, or a grapevine figs? Neither can a salt spring furnish fresh water.

THE COVENANT

PRESERVING POWER

SALT AND FLOUR

ARE YOU SEASONED WELL?

SALTY

FLAVORED WITH PURPOSE

GRACE FLAVOR

NO LOOKING BACK

NO TRUE SAVOR

TASTELESS

PROMISE TO PRESERVE

THE COVENANT

Numbers 18:1 (NKJV)

"All the heave offerings of the holy things, which the children of Israel offer to the LORD, I have given to you and your sons and daughters with you as an ordinance forever; it is a covenant of salt forever before the LORD with you and your descendants with you."

Covenant

The conditional promises made to humanity by God, as revealed in Scripture. The agreement God made to ancient Israelites, in which God promised to protect them if they kept His law and were faithful to Him.

The Salt Covenant is the most extraordinary promise given to us from the "Promise Keeper." With this covenant, God promises endurance, preservation, and freedom from corruption. This covenant should perpetually remind us of His faithfulness in our life. Salt like the rainbow, is a sign of our Creator's oath to us. Even the holy ingredients used for the incense were to have salt added, (Exodus 30:35). You shall make of this incense, a compound according to the art of the perfumer, salted, pure, *and* holy. Sodium regulates the passage of nutrients into the cells. Without salt, nutrients cannot enter your cells and will become malnourished and exhausted no matter how good you believe your diet to be. Without our Creator's pledge, we would be spiritually starved and morally exhausted. Salt represents an unbreakable covenant. The scripture above says *"forever,"* can you find anything in this world today that has this eternal quality? We are quick to throw away things. However, our eternal God is in the preservation business. God considers us His greatest masterpiece. We are His special creation so He put in His plan a maintenance protection strategy for us. God made a covenant agreement with David, that his family would rule Israel forever. (2 Chron.13:5) The covenant stands in Jesus Christ. Jesus has dominion over Israel forever. There is an eternal blessing to a Salt Covenant. When

God made a covenant with David… it was all up to God to fulfill His promise. Jesus came from the lineage of David through both Mary and Joseph. By His death, He became the salted sacrifice offered before God to cleanse the people from their sin: not for a moment, but for all time. It is infinitely attainable to all who will accept His provision of cleansing and forgiveness. It does not just cover the sin, but it removes it. It is a binding contract that God made on our behalf….How salty is your life; does it reflect that you are fully aware of the covenant God ordained with peace, love, and grace?

"This Salt Contract, can never be revoked,
it is from the Promise Keeper."

PRESERVING POWER

John 17:11-12 (NKJV)

Now I am no longer in the world, but these are in the world, and I come to You. Holy Father, keep through Your name those whom You have given Me, that they may be one as We are. While I was with them in the world, I kept them in Your name. Those whom You gave Me I have kept; and none of them is lost except the son of perdition, that the Scripture might be fulfilled.

"I kept them in Your name," is a comment loaded with love. In Bible times, a name stood for its owner's essential character. When the Father gave His name to the Son, He commissioned Him to act with His authority and power. This scripture represents the staying power of a name. At first glance, Jesus wanted the disciples to be united in harmony just like the Father, Son, and Holy Spirit. Jesus further explains that He kept them, stating His preserving power sustained each one of them. Without it, all would be lost or doomed like Judas. **Preserve** means; to keep safe from harm or injury; protect or spare. The preserving power of Christ that spared us is absolutely the best fire protection insurance we could own. Look at five advantages such coverage offers. 1. Secured salvation. 2. Triumph over Satan's devised plots. 3. The Word esteems us. 4. Harmony with God and others. 5. Lionize with GOD in heaven. Can you imagine your life without this preserving power? I cannot bear to think about it, because it all comes down to this one truth. This preserving power is what keeps us as believers protected from the evil schemes of Satan. Jesus had a worldwide vision, in His vision He desired that we would all come to know Him. Once we conceded, His blood would preserve us until that faithful day: when He returns to take us home to be with Him.

"The blood of Christ has preserved our life."

SALT AND FLOUR

2 Kings 2:19-23 (NKJV)

Then the men of the city said to Elisha, "Please notice, the situation of this city is pleasant, as my lord sees; but the water is bad, and the ground barren." And he said, "Bring me a new bowl, and put salt in it." So they brought it to him. Then he went out to the source of the water, and cast in the salt there, and said, "Thus says the LORD: 'I have healed this water; from it there shall be no more death or barrenness." So the water remains healed to this day, according to the word of Elisha which he spoke.

God, in His infinite power, can do all things in any manner He chooses. He is God. While God could have healed the waters in a different manner, the clean new bowl and the salt were the appropriate symbols of purification, preservation, and holiness. The word "barren," proves there was no harvest in the land. Water (Holy Spirit) is needed to help things grow, producing a good, healthy harvest. In the book of Leviticus, God gave us a covenantal contract that would keep us preserved as His children. In all four Gospels, we see that we are the "salt" of the earth, which illustrates we are the chosen life preservers. There are several ingredients stocked in your pantry that God uses in His Word, to allow us to see that He is all-powerful and nothing in life is beyond His control, not even death. 2 Kings 4:38-41 (NKJV) states, "And Elisha returned to Gilgal, and *there was* a famine in the land. Now the sons of the prophets *were* sitting before him; and he said to his servant, "Put on the large pot, and boil stew for the sons of the prophets." So one went out into the field to gather herbs, and found a wild vine, and gathered from it a lapful of wild gourds, and came and sliced *them* into the pot of stew, though they did not know *what they were*. Then they served it to the men to eat. Now it happened, as they were eating the stew, that they cried out and said, "Man of God, *there is* death in the pot!" And they could not eat *it*. So he said, "Then bring some flour." And he put *it* into the pot, and said, "Serve *it* to the people, that they may eat." And there was no death in the pot.

"Salt, Flour, and Water in my hands are just ingredients".
"Salt, Flour and Water in the Master's hands are life preserving."

ARE YOU SEASONED WELL?

Leviticus 2:13 (ESV)

You shall season all your grain offerings with salt. You shall not let the salt of the covenant with your God be missing from your grain offering; with all your offerings you shall offer salt.

Besides worship and praise, our other assignment on earth is to witness to others. We are to witness in a way that will pique interest for others to know the amazing God we serve. Food at a restaurant can make or break your mood for fun. If your entrée is not what you expected, you can be irritated and downright ready to run for the nearest exit, especially if it is cold or possibly burned. If the seasoning is not right, forget about it. Well, just as the text above states, with all your offerings you shall offer salt. Of course you should! Just like your food, if not seasoned well who wants fancy or appealing vittles. Salt is the preserving factor in what we consume, have you tasted the foods that say low-sodium, BORING? I purpose not to be a low-sodium believer. Consider the shelves at the super-market during the holiday season. If you are a last minute shopper, the canned goods you need for your nine-course meal, will either be labeled "low-sodium" or "no salt" by the time you get there. Whether ministering on the streets, in a pulpit, or maybe even on a plane, please be sure that you are seasoned just right. You want those that get a taste to desire more of the flavor, after you've introduced them to Christ. Do not be left on the shelf.

"Please pass the salt."

SALTY

James 3:11-12 (ESV)

Does a spring pour forth from the same opening both fresh and salt water? Can a fig tree, my brothers, bear olives, or a grapevine produce figs? Neither can a salt pond yield fresh water.

Watch what you say about others. "Sticks and stones may break my bones, but words can never hurt me." Ludicrous! Words are so important and loaded with power. Why else would Solomon say, "life and death is in the power of the tongue?" Too much of anything is not good for you. While traveling with my publisher and two dear friends, we were famished, not familiar with the area we drove till something looked familiar. In unison, all but one of us screamed "WHAT-A-BURGER!©" It's the name of a southern burger chain. Did I say we considered ourselves starved? Well 4 cheeseburgers, 2 onion rings, 4 medium drinks, and 5 fries later. OK, something does not add up, we have 1 french-fry too many. I said we were hungry. Over the drive-thru speaker, we hear, "Any condiments?" We all shout in unison, "Salt." I often wonder why everyone asks for salt, and then apply it without first tasting. My experience has been when servers forget to ask if we need condiments, there is never enough salt on the food. However, we were overloaded with far too many salt packets than four people could use. They had actually over-salted the food. Willa, gasps aloud, "Oh my, this is salty." However, once the salt has been applied, just like words, you cannot take them back. Remember being a kid and the wrong words slipped from your immature lips? Your tongue becomes acquainted with Ivory™ soap, and after a few glasses of water; the soap residue is gone. Have you ever tried to rinse or rub salt off french-fries that have been drenched in too much salt? Salt sticks to its applied subject, just like words. Therefore, you must remember the words of our mothers, "If you don't have anything nice to say, don't say anything at all."

"Words seasoned with salt always taste good to the hearer."

FLAVORED WITH PURPOSE

Mark 9:50 (KJV)

Salt is good, but if the salt loses its flavor, how will you season it? Have salt in yourselves, and have peace with one another."

Jesus used this mineral to teach us the characteristic of what His followers must exhibit. He considers us beneficial in His goal. Jesus'candid approach was for us to focus directly and remember God's faithfulness. Just as salt was used when making a sacrifice, He recalled God's covenant with His people. Jesus also illustrates here that we are to make a difference in the flavor of the world, just as salt changes food's flavor. His message is distinct; our purpose is to counteract the moral decay in society. As a preservative, salt prevents food from spoiling. When we choose not to "salt" the earth with God's love and His Word, we are useless to Him. We must remember there are lives attached to us for the proper seasoning. The God we serve is sovereign, loving, and kind: doing all things on purpose with each of us in mind. His goal is that none whom He created perishes. The allegory used here by our parable-teaching Savior was to solicit our partnership in this deteriorating world. He knows this that world lacks an adequate supply of this mineral essential to preserve and cultivate life. The prerequisite is solid and to the point. Zest, savor, gusto, and a whole lot of zing are required in your life's recipe as a believer. Each ingredient is imperative for achieving the desired flavor of the life He designed when He wrote the perfect plan.

"The flavor of life needs more than a pinch of Salt."

GRACE FLAVOR

Colossians 4:6 (NKJV)

Let your speech always be with grace, seasoned with salt, that you may know how you ought to answer each one.

If we have grace in our hearts, it will be evident in our speech. In this letter to the Colossians, Paul illustrates the necessity of having tasteful and gracious communication with each other. Salt is a metaphor for Christian conversation. Therefore, it improves taste, and when our words are seasoned with grace it is easier for the listener to digest. Salt we know is also a preservative. Consequently; when we do our God-given part, which is to preach salvation through the Gospel of Jesus Christ, someone's life is preserved from death!. Paul also emphasizes our responsibility to help create a thirst in the lives of a non-believers, as well as believers. Just as popcorn or salty treats create thirst; our gracious speech should spark a desire from our listener. We should live a life of compassion coupled with honesty and true grace. Outside of this we are condoning their present spoiling. Or we can say; we are cheering their steps with our salt-less ruin.

"Our gracious flavor is purposed to help recover a decaying life."

NO LOOKING BACK

Genesis 19:26 (KJV)

But his wife looked back from behind him,
and she became a pillar of salt.

Moses pegged this one right. There are consequences we must face when we do not listen intently to the warnings the Lord has decreed for our good. The Lord instructs Moses to gather the people and speak to the rock. Moses' not following directions was a little nervy. He speaks to the people and hits the rock instead. For his punishment, Moses loses entry into the Promised Land. Now consider Lott, Abraham's nephew. Due to the unrighteousness in Sodom and Gomorrah, Lott's family was informed by Angels sent from the Lord, "to escape for their lives quickly and not to look back." Lott's wife looked back. Immediately, she turned into a pillar of salt. Yikes! I propose that the Lord made her "salt," in her death what she should have been while she lived. Visualize if Lott's wife would have been salting the land with God's love and His word. Quite possibly, Sodom and Gomorrah may have not been so corrupt. Her fate is a warning to those who may prefer the pleasures of this earthly life, rather than the blessings of God's kingdom. Looking back at the life God had just delivered her from, ended in a fatal demise for Lott's wife! When we vacillate, from salty to unsalted, we are no different. Jesus refers to her ruin in the Gospel of Luke, forewarning us that by looking back we risk forfeiting our gracious departure.

"A Salty life takes time to season and
preserve lives that are salt-less."

NO TRUE SAVOR

Luke 14:34 (NKJV)

"Salt is good; but if the salt has lost its flavor, how shall it be seasoned?

While percolating over this very salty question, I have come to a resolve. Real salt does not lose its flavor. Nonetheless it can be diluted. However, we do agree the perception subliminally etched out here is pointing its salty pointer at you and I. Another way of politely asking, "Zeal is good; but if the zeal loses its fire, how does one get it back?" Do you remember the person that first introduced you to Christ? Imagine, if there was no distinctive saltiness, in other words, if they were not set apart from your usual crew in fact they looked just like them. Salt has two explicit functions in the life of a believer. One purpose is to add flavor. Ponder a moment before this mineral was part of our lives, we were lifeless, a tad bit tasteless and destined for a bland unfulfilling life. Another specific purpose for this tasty mineral is to preserve. Yes, we are the mouthpieces in the earth that God carefully chose to assist in the preservation lost souls. What an assignment? If we lose our savory flavor, many would spoil. Every circumstance we have overcome, we should discreetly season with the intent to help another. Being "salty" is not easy, but is essential if we are going to follow God's original plan. He desires to get all who are spoiling back to Him. We must use our God-given mineral to salt the earth. Our greatest example is Jesus Christ. He went to the cross to ensure our preservation. One quick note: the human body cannot survive without Salt…It's the salt that helps maintain your blood's water balance.

"Time to Savor your Flavor, a life depends on it."

TASTELESS

Job 6:6 (NKJV)

Can flavorless food be eaten without salt? Or is there any taste in the white of an egg?

Job was fed up. He was distressed, sick, and tired. Job's friends were giving him advice, and it was last thing he needed. Eliphaz's opinion to Job was like eating bland food: such as the white of an egg. When people are in the midst of a turbulent storm, ill-advised counsel is distasteful. Oftentimes, we listen intently, however we are screaming on the inside "get out of my face." James tells us to be swift to hear and slow to speak, and slow to wrath. Good advice. Taking this course of action will decrease the chances of a brawl. Most people assume that if there is a trial you must have done something wrong. They also assume that this is God's way of punishing you. These tasteless believers must have forgotten the benevolence of our God. I say "believers" simply because for them to blame God, they must also believe in Him. Our suffering may not be the result of sin in our life. Nonetheless, we must be careful not to become tasteless, and allow our suffering to cause us to sin. Jesus had an interesting response when asked by the disciples about a blind man who sinned. Was it this man or his parents? Jesus answered, "Neither this man nor his parents sinned, but that the works of God should be revealed in him. I must work the works of Him who sent Me while it is day; *the* night is coming when no one can work." Boom. It's proven by the "Way Maker" that trials come to make us stronger. Once we have been enlightened, we are to salt the earth. In order for us to remain salty, we should intentionally follow the advice James has given us. Remember, God knows what He is doing in all of our lives. Choosing our words wisely to season only what needs to have seasoning added to it is critical. It determines the taste left on your palate as well as your dining guest.

"Do not be like the white of an egg, choose to season wisely."

PROMISE TO PRESERVE

Psalm 119:50 (NIV)

My comfort in my suffering is this:
Your promise preserves my life.

When you feel as though you are decaying in this spoiling and corrupt world, focus on a few promising Psalms. The scriptures were written for our benefit as a reminder of the contract that includes you. David, the writer of Psalms, experienced firsthand the preserving power of God.
(*the following translations are NKJV*)

Psalm 121:7 ~ The LORD shall preserve you from all evil; He shall preserve your soul.

Psalm 64:1 ~ Hear my voice, O God, in my meditation; Preserve my life from fear of the enemy.

Psalm 121:8 ~ The LORD shall preserve your going out and your coming in. From this time forth, and even forevermore.

Psalm 32:7 ~ You are my hiding place; You shall preserve me from trouble; You shall surround me with songs of deliverance. ***Selah***

Psalm 145:20 ~ The LORD preserves all who love Him. But all the wicked He will destroy.

Psalm 140:4 ~ Keep me, O LORD, from the hands of the wicked; Preserve me from violent men, Who have purposed to make my steps stumble.

Psalm 116:6 ~ The LORD preserves the simple; I was brought low, and He saved me.

Psalm 40:11 ~ Do not withhold your tender mercies from me, O LORD; Let Your loving-kindness and Your truth continually preserve me.

"Our Father's predetermined Will, that we are all PRESERVED."

EPISODE EIGHT

YES IT'S SUFFICIENT

2nd Corinthians 12:9 (NKJV)

And He said to me, "My grace is sufficient for you, for My strength is made perfect in weakness."

AXIOMS OF PROVERBS

ONE WEEK

CHANGE FRIENDS

WORDS WITH FRENZ

SHADOW OF CHRIST

THAT BRAIN

LIBERTY & JUSTICE

HE SO LOVED

THIS GREAT TRUTH

EXTRAVAGANT IS THIS GIFT

PRAYER OF SALVATION

AXIOMS OF PROVERBS

Proverbs 1:8-9 (NKJV)

My son, hear the instruction of thy father,
and forsake not the law of thy mother:
For they shall be an ornament of grace unto thy head,
and chains about thy neck.

Axiom: a self-evident truth that requires no proof.

Proverbs 3:22
They will be life for you, an ornament to **grace** your neck.

Proverbs 3:34
Surely he scorneth the scorners: but he giveth grace unto the lowly.

Proverbs 4:9
She shall give to thine head an ornament of grace: a crown of glory shall she deliver to thee.

Proverbs 22:11
He that loveth pureness of heart, for the grace of his lips the king shall be his friend.

"Wisdom is led by Grace for insight to always do what is right."

ONE WEEK

Monday
Mandatory
Obedience
Necessary
Devotion
Adds abundance
Yield

Tuesday
Temptation
Unchecked
Eventually
Stifles
Devoted
Anointed vessels
Yaw (to distract or take off course)

Wednesday
Worship
Enables
Daily blessings
New revelations
Enriching
Strength
Divine favor
Abundance from
Yahweh

Thursday
Today
He
Undoubtedly
Rewards
Sincere
Dedication
And Allots
You ~ grace

Friday
Favor
Reveals
Immanuel's
Deep desire &
Adoration for
You

Saturday
Salvation
Acquits
Thoughts
Under
Rejection
Delivers
A VICTORY to
You

Sunday
Standing
Uprightly
Nourishes
Deliverance
Always
Yeah Mon

"7 days without prayer makes 1 weak, however seven days without grace equals death."

CHANGE FRIENDS

Matthew 6:34 (AMP)

So do not worry or be anxious about tomorrow, for tomorrow will have worries and anxieties of its own. Sufficient for each day is its own trouble.

They are all very good friends, and it's no coincidence they live on the same dead-end street, Nagging Drive. Let me introduce them to you: Ms. Worry, Mr. Stress, Lady Anxiety, Mrs. Headache, Mr. & Mrs. Panic and their daughter Sleep Deprived. Clearly, they have never read the passage where the Savior told his worrisome disciples that worry had no real benefits. In fact, it was so meaningless that it could not even add a millisecond to their life spans. It really is a funny thing about those we chose to keep in our company. If you like the state you're in, look closely around you. Chances are, you'll see in your circle of friends that have the same heart, along with similar interests and positive thoughts. Unfortunately, somewhere along the journey, the friends became consumed with negative thoughts. They missed the right turn to get them home in a timely manner. Instead they took an altered left at the intersection of Confusion Parkway. This wrong turn cost them time, energy and unwanted anguish. Considering what has been written, let me ask you this question. Which person can you identify with in this sad company of friends? They were walking very closely with me: during the time my Mother took ill right after our Holiday. While I know Jehovah-Ropha would answer according to His will, the problem was I forgot that His will is what the blood accomplished. All are healed by the stripes of Jesus. So I guess it would be safe for me to admit that I was closely communicating with all six families in the neighborhood at the same time. In fact, I had them on speed-dial on my mobile phone. I understand Jesus was directing the worrywarts that were in His Company that worry is worthless and unnecessary. Therefore, after moments of unnecessary worthlessness were still part of my familiar crew, I finally went to my husband. I asked, "What are your thoughts" Ron softly replied "I don't control the next minute. All I have right now is this moment, and in it I chose to see your Mother smile, relax and get better." Not satisfied, I ask a very dear friend the same question. Gena replied, "I am not going to speculate. But will say this, it is in tests like this when we prove our faith." Lips shut, I choose these two friends, Mr. Calm & Ms. Faith, because the nagging others were making me sick after-all.

"There is a Friend that sticks closer than a brother, I pray you know ***Him****."*

WORDS WITH FRENZ

Mark 16:15 (NIV)

He said to them, "Go into all the world and preach the gospel to all creation.

I call her Aussie Jo, We met through a word game over the Internet. We had been playing for about 3 days before she politely asked where I lived and how old I was. I thought that was an odd question, however, I quickly replied "I'm in California." She responded, I'm in Sydney Australia. Wow! Initially, I thought this could be a fraud. I asked if she was on Facebook™ so I could see if she was who she represented herself to be. Her reply was, "not yet." I nerved up for just a tad and stopped responding only to have her ask, again how old I was and what did I do in Cali. Then she proceeded to sing through the words she was writing, "I wish they all could be California girls" by the Beach Boys. Little did we know that the Father in heaven had orchestrated this divine connection which is a very long but a beautiful story. I will make it as short as possible. When I replied I was a writer working on my third edition of the series, she did her own investigating through the amazing internet and quickly replied, "Oh my God you're a Minister, and this is freaking me out." Shocked by her reply, I took a moment to respond, my reply was simple, I like what I do. Aussie went on to tell her story; her parents were devout Christians, she could not remember if she had ever spoken to God on her own. As if things could not be worse, she had been dating an Atheist for the past ten years that she had recently ended. By the way, I asked her permission to share this phenomenal story. Aussie Jo shared further that on this particular night, she had been to a dance class with some girlfriends, she was so elated, that on her way into her high-rise apartment she glanced up to the sky only to 'THANK GOD for the peace she finally felt.' Two hours later, we met. My heart raced, as I began to search for words to explain how special to the she is to the Father, that on the other side world, He would coordinate our connection so that she would know that He heard her sincere THANK

YOU." Aussie Jo, blessed my life on many levels. We talk now 2 to 3 times a week, and most importantly, she not only prays but also attends church. I am a member of Living Praise Christian Center in Chatsworth, California. Aussie Jo now attends Living Praise Christian Centre in Chatswood, Australia. He is strategic, absolutely no coincidences when it comes to our Loving Father.

Hi Theresa,
I am so glad to have met you through words with friends and a little help from God also :)
your new Aussie friend.
Jo

"Wednesday 7:00 am in California, and 2:00 am Thursday in Australia mission accomplished."

SHADOW OF CHRIST

James 1:17 (KJV)

Every good gift and every perfect gift is from above, and cometh down from the Father of lights, with whom is no variableness, neither shadow of turning.

The Old Testament scriptures provide us with many "shadows", or "types," that have remarkable similarities to our Lord Jesus Christ and the events of His life. These similarities confirm that the plan for our Lord Jesus Christ was determined long before the events of His ministry. These shadows also stand as evidence that Jesus Christ truly is the Messiah, and the ancient prophets foretold what would come. Among these shadows are (1) the brazen serpent, (2) Isaac, the son of Abraham, (3) Joseph, the son of Jacob, (4) Jonah, the prophet, (5) the scapegoat, (6) the sacrificial Passover lamb, and (7) the rock, which Moses struck. Consider the following:

- Both Joseph and Jesus Christ were beloved of their fathers. The Father says of Jesus Christ, "... This is my beloved Son, in whom I am well pleased ...."
- Both were sold by their brethren, Joseph was sold into slavery for 20 pieces of silver. Jesus Christ was betrayed for 30 pieces of silver.
- Joseph was thrown into prison, Jesus Christ was placed into a tomb.
- Joseph emerged from the prison to be exalted to the right hand of Pharaoh. Jesus Christ rose from the dead to be exalted to the right hand of the Father. "Then Pharaoh sent and called Joseph, and they brought him hastily out of the dungeon ..." (Genesis 41:14, NKJV). "And Pharaoh said unto Joseph, Forasmuch as God hath shewed thee all this, there is none so discreet and wise as thou art: Thou shalt be over my house, and according unto thy

word shall all my people be ruled: only in the throne will I be greater than thou ... I have set thee over all the land of Egypt." This foreshadowed what Jesus Christ would do when He rose from the dead and was exalted to the right hand of God. Ephesians 1:18-20 (NKJV) says, "The eyes of your understanding being enlightened; that ye may know ... the exceeding greatness of his power toward us who believe ... Which he worked in Christ, when he raised him from the dead, and set him at his own right hand in the heavenly places."

- Joseph received a virgin bride after being exalted. Jesus Christ will receive a church (Bride) without spot or blemish. Paul says in 2 Corinthians 11:2 (NKJV), "... I have **espoused** you to one husband that I may present you as a **chaste virgin** to Christ."
- Joseph received his virgin bride during the time of rejection by his brothers and before a great famine. Similarly, Jesus Christ will get His bride while being rejected by Israel and before the great tribulation.
- Through Joseph, God saved not only Egypt and Israel, but all the nations of the world from starvation during the seven-year famine. This foreshadowed Jesus Christ becoming the "bread of life" for a world, which was hopelessly lost. "And Jesus said unto them, I am the **bread of life**: he that cometh to me shall never hunger; and he that believeth on me shall never thirst." (John 6:35, NKJV). Paul writes in 1 Corinthians 10:16-17, "... The **bread** which we break, is it not the communion of the **body of Christ**? For we being many are one bread, and one body: for we are all partakers of that one bread."
- Although Joseph knew his brothers at their first meeting, they did not recognize him until they met the second time. Likewise, Israel will not recognize Jesus Christ until He comes to them for the second time.
- God had Joseph sold into slavery so that he could eventually save all his brothers. This was a shadow of the sacrifice made by Jesus Christ, the Messiah, was put to death to save the world

Joseph forgave his brothers who sold him into slavery. Likewise, Jesus Christ forgave His brethren who crucified Him, saying "...

Father, forgive them; for they know not what they do ..." (Luke 23:34, NKJV).

- These striking similarities demonstrate that the plan for the life, death, resurrection, and ascension of our Lord Jesus Christ were ordained from the beginning of time. This foreshadowing stands as evidence that Jesus Christ is who He said He is, the Son of God.

"Joseph saved his brothers, Jesus Christ saved you."

THAT BRAIN

Job 33:4 (KJV)

The spirit of God hath made me, and the breath of the Almighty hath given me life.

Here we are in the UCLA Mattel Children's Hospital Pediatrics Ward. Our son is the patient. I had to ask God several times, "Are you serious?" There were so many "Why's" I forgot the count. While sitting on the makeshift bed I created, I asked God at least one more time. "Why?" The monitors are going off as if they had a significant purpose. Beep! Beep! I am done! There is no explanation. No reason to disturb what I consider my quiet moment. Nevertheless, the "beeps" continue. Therefore, I decide to ask the Master, not the doctor, "What's up?" Faithful to His Word to answer quickly, God reminded me to look at Jaylon's request for the doctor to answer a few questions of concern. The first on Jaylon's list, "How long will my speech be like this?" He had what the doctors call a "Cavernous Malformation," therefore resembling a stroke. Need I say more? Jaylon was 14 at the time, and wanted to know when he would get his "swag back." You know his swagger to chat. In a very audible voice, I heard God say, "read Job 33." Instantly, the revelation jumped from the page and into my heart. God said, "I made it, so I know how it functions." It was Dr. Marie's answer to J's question. "Your brain will correct your speech." With tear-filled eyes, I understood that God was telling me the same thing the doctor said. "I Am the Brain. I correct what is wrong in the body." My mind was put at ease simply because He answered swiftly to this inquisitive Mother's plea for understanding. The Godhead is the Ultimate Brain, ~Father ~Son, and Holy Ghost.

Isaiah 53:5 (KJV)

But he was wounded for our transgressions, he was bruised for our iniquities: the chastisement of our peace was upon him; and with his **stripes** *we are healed.*

"By the stripes of Jesus Christ we are Healed."

LIBERTY & JUSTICE

2 Corinthians 3:17 (NKJV)

Now the Lord is the Spirit; and where the Spirit of the Lord is, there is liberty.

Liberty: freedom from control, interference, obligation, restriction, hampering conditions, etc.; power or right of doing, thinking, speaking, etc., according to choice. Free from captivity, confinement, or physical restraint:

New York has the Statue of Liberty; Philadelphia has the Liberty Bell, then there is the Pledge of Allegiance that declares, "…Liberty & Justice for all." The Lord is Spirit, The Holy Spirit is God, Himself, like the Father and like the Son. Liberty from our Lord grants us justice, grace, and mercy. It gives us freedom over death and condemnation of the law. Can you imagine your life without liberty? This liberty is another way of saying free will. God has given us two options. This liberty says in a boisterous manner: it is either life or death. You can willfully take this sufficient grace or live graceless. Liberty & Justice have declared us as freely justified under the Blood of Calvary. In the United States of America's, pledge, it states "Liberty and Justice for all." Jesus' blood has a promise that includes everyone that's not based on race, color, or creed. This profound declaration was granted to all who would be willing to accept such an extravagant gift when Jesus said, "I love you this much." Then, He stretched on a rugged cross: one arm to the right the other to the left, took His last breath and died for us. Not being restricted to the grave on the third day, He rose again, and so goes this liberty. For where the Spirit of the Lord is there is LIBERTY. So glad I am free are you?

"Liberty, and Justice for all who come to Him."

HE SO LOVED

Ephesians 3:9-10 (NKJV)

And to make all men see what is the fellowship of the mystery, which from the beginning of the world hath been hid in God, who created all things by Jesus Christ: To the intent that now unto the principalities and powers in heavenly places might be known by the church the manifold wisdom of God.

This verse yields amazing insight into God's purposes with respect to His angelic creation. Both Holy angels and the fallen angels who have followed Satan in his age-long rebellion against God have access to wisdom. They were intently observing and learning about God, His nature, and His purpose through God's work of creating and redeeming all men and women. The church, and the vast body of redeemed individuals, past and present, is serving as an instructor to the angels. Also being taught are those angels assigned as our individual guardians and ministers. What does salvation mean to you? Why did God give us such phenomenal gifts? Salvation according to the scripture written by Paul has been a hidden mystery since the beginning of the world. The prophets of old, including Moses, had a desire to look into Salvation. However, they were not offered this great salvation gift. Their ability to be atoned for sins was through the sacrifice of bulls and lambs. In the end, Jesus was the perfect unblemished Lamb. He was slain once for all our sins, past, present, and future. Luke 2:25-30 (NKJV) states, "And, behold, there was a man in Jerusalem, whose name was Simeon; and the same man was just and devout, waiting for the consolation of Israel: and the Holy Ghost was upon him. And it was revealed unto him by the Holy Ghost, that he should not see death, before he had seen the Lord's Christ. And he came by the Spirit into the temple: and when the parents brought in the child Jesus, to do for him after the custom of the law. Then took he him up in his arms, and blessed God, and said, Lord, now lettest thou thy servant depart in peace, according to thy word: For mine eyes have seen thy salvation." Simeon saw through the Holy Spirit that the infant in his arms would bring salvation both to the Jews and Gentiles. The Bible first mentions "salvation" in Genesis 49:18. Jacob said that he was "waiting" for it to come. Simeon, his son, would actually witness this "grand gift" in the person of the young Jesus. Simeon held Jesus in arms, and therefore declared, "For mine eyes have seen thy salvation." John 3:16 (NKJV) reminds us, "God so loved the world that He gave His only begotten Son that whosoever believes in Him should not perish but have everlasting life."

Do you believe?

THIS GREAT TRUTH

John 14:6 (KJV)

Jesus saith unto him, I am the way, the truth, and the life: no man cometh unto the Father, but by me.

Salvation is indeed a great truth! The very name of "Jesus" means salvation. It embraces many major doctrines of scripture such as; atonement (Leviticus 17:11), substitution (Isaiah 53:5) imputation (Romans 4:6-8), propitiation (1 John 2:2), redemption (1Peter 1:18), remission (Acts 10:43), Justification (Romans 3:28), adoption (Ephesians 1:5), reconciliation (Romans 5:10-11), regeneration (Titus 3:5), sanctification (2 Thessalonians 2:13), and glorification (Romans 8:30). Salvation is the most precious gift God has granted all humanity. Jesus said no man could see the Father unless they first know Him. Jesus is our Salvation. He is our ticket to everlasting life, and the Way Maker. The Angels declare, "Who is man that thou art mindful of him, the Son of Man visits him? It is important to God that all He created come to the knowledge of salvation." (Titus 2:11, NKJV) states, "For the grace of God that bringeth salvation hath appeared to all men." God has ensured that all men will be made aware of the power of God in creation (Romans 1:20) and the grace of God in salvation (Acts 14:17). Therefore, they are without excuse. Men and women should know there is a God of all creation who makes provision for life. Nonetheless, He is also the same God that must invoke the wages (payment) of "sin." (Romans 6:23, NKJV) "For the wages of sin *is* death, but the gift of God *is* eternal life in Christ Jesus our Lord." God designated Jesus as the Savior of the world. Thus, there is no other that can be His equal. He is our Salvation. (Acts 4:12) Nor is there any other type of salvation. There is no other name under heaven given among men by which we must be saved." (2 Corinthians 7:10) Godly sorrow produces repentance leading to salvation, not to be regretted; but the sorrow of the world produces death. Godly sorrow is a change in behavior, which leads to true repentance, turning us back to God. He can give us spiritual deliverance. Worldly sorrow produces death. (Hebrews 2:3) How shall we escape if we neglect so great a salvation, which at first began to be spoken by the Lord? This redemption was confirmed to us by those who heard Him. Ponder a moment on three nails, a crown of thorns, rugged cross, the blood, and sword that pierced our Lord's side. Five is the number of grace; these five critical elements were used for our Salvation to be rendered, which in the end grants us exclusive GRACE.

For Jesus, the nails meant your life.

EXTRAVAGANT IS THIS GIFT

John 3:16 (KJV)

For God so loved the world, that he gave his only begotten Son, that whosoever believeth in him should not perish, but have everlasting life.

In Romans, Paul tells us that Christ died for us while we were yet still sinners. In Psalms, David illustrates that the loving God sought us out. The Bible tells us in Titus 3; salvation was being freely given to them that believed. Therefore it is not given because of our works, or good deeds. Rather, because we just believe in the regeneration and renewing of the Holy Spirit. My own experience with this amazing God was certainly life-changing. I'm positive you can say the same, if you know Him as Lord. Other words to explain this life-changing gift are; Rescued; Pardoned; Restored; Released; Delivered; Emancipated; Acquitted and Justified. God leaves no doubt about our condition. While we set our standards of right and wrong by society's values, God's standard is His own holiness. He said to, "Be holy for He is Holy," (1 Peter 3:16). How do we measure up? "For all have sinned and come short of the glory of God," (Romans 3:23). In His infinite wisdom, it is only reasonable that God demand and require holiness; which was His original created plan for our lives He designed. However, since the fall of Adam in the garden, we have rebelled against Him as a race and as individuals. Our sin issues separate us from God. The moment He bore OUR sins on the cross, and cried out, "Why have thou forsaken me," sin separated Jesus from His Father. Because sin puts us in darkness and God is light, He cannot go against His own created order. Nevertheless, God loves us so much that He would turn the earth upside down and inside out to reach the ones He loves. After all, He sent His Son to die for us. Our sin has brought its consequences. There is no mercy in suffering, no freedom from bondage, no lasting joy, and no hope for the future. Terminal is the life that is without SALVATION. The repercussions of sin are eternal separation from our gracious Father. We need redemption from our sin, from its bondage, and from its great unending consequences. This salvation plan is not limited to any living being, but is available to all. God has a predetermined will for His greatest masterpieces in the earth. For this purpose alone, the Lamb of God was slain before He created earth's foundation. God's perfect strategy was His gift of Salvation to get us back to Him.

"God's greatest Gift redeemed our life."

PRAYER OF SALVATION

Romans 10:9 (KJV)

That if thou shalt confess with thy mouth the Lord Jesus, and shalt believe in thine heart that God hath raised him from the dead, thou shalt be saved.

Father, I confess that I am a sinner. I ask that You would come into my heart and save me. That You would give me the opportunity to live eternally with You. I recognize that Jesus Christ is Your only begotten son. That He willfully died for my sins that I may be cleansed from all unrighteousness. Lord, I thank You for my salvation, and also for Your grace and daily mercies. You are awesome to Love me as You do, and for this I will bless Your name forever. Create in me a new heart, and renew a steadfast spirit within me. That I may live an acceptable life that will be pleasing to You until You return. As I rejoice for my new life, I understand that all the Angels in heaven rejoice, along with me. Jesus, thank You for the Blood that from this moment will cover my life and keep me safe from the snares of the wicked one.
Amen

2 Corinthians 6:2 (KJV)

(For he saith, I have heard thee in a time accepted, and in the day of salvation have I succored thee: behold, now is the accepted time; behold, now is the day of salvation.)

REFERENCES USED

King James Version (KJV)

New King James Version (NKJV)

English Standard Version (ESV)

New International Version (NIV)

Today's New International Version (TNIV)

Message (MSG)

Amplified Version (AMP)

Contemporary English Version (CEV)

God's Word Translation (GWT)

Holman Christian Standard Bible (HCSB)

Dictionary.com, LLC - Copyright©2010

Roget's 21st Century Thesaurus, Third Edition
Copyright©2010

ABOUT THE AUTHOR

Theresa A. Kirk is a wife, mother, sister, minister of the Gospel of Jesus Christ, author, speaker, and a friend to many. Theresa acknowledges the call on her life for this season. She has a burning desire to minister to the Body of Christ. However, her heart is especially fixed towards the ministry of women. Theresa has been active in ministry for most of her life, but she gives a heartfelt confession that she has not always lived a born-again life. God gained her attention one night, more than 15 years ago, while attending a women's conference. She later confessed to a friend that she was captivated by the women on the platform and that is what she would like to do. Theresa described the women as funny, sensitive and yet all were power-packed with the Word of God. Little did she know that the season she spoke so fondly of would present itself as a reality. She testifies that the Lord opened a door and because of her desire to do His will, she accepted the call. She gave the Lord a complete, YES. Theresa is grateful for the awesome leadership, ministering and teaching of her Pastors, Dr. Fred and Linda Hodge of Living Praise Christian Center of Chatsworth and Lancaster, California. Her close friends have coined her as the modern day "Paul." They witness that she receives "revelation upon revelation." It has been prophesied that just like Paul, God will bring her speak before Kings.

Theresa is the author of the ***Some Things Made Plain***, a four volume book series. Volume 1, ***Some Things Made Plain*** and Volume 2, ***W.O.R.D. ~ Wisdom's Oil Released Daily***, were released in 2011. Volume 3, This Explicit Grace-Yes It's Sufficient will be released in Fall 2012. Volume 4, It's That Simple is due to be released in Winter 2013.

She is married to Ron W. Kirk, and they have two amazing children, Chelsea and Jaylon and they live in Palmdale, California.

NOTES

NOTES

NOTES

The
SOME THINGS MADE PLAIN
Series
By Theresa Kirk

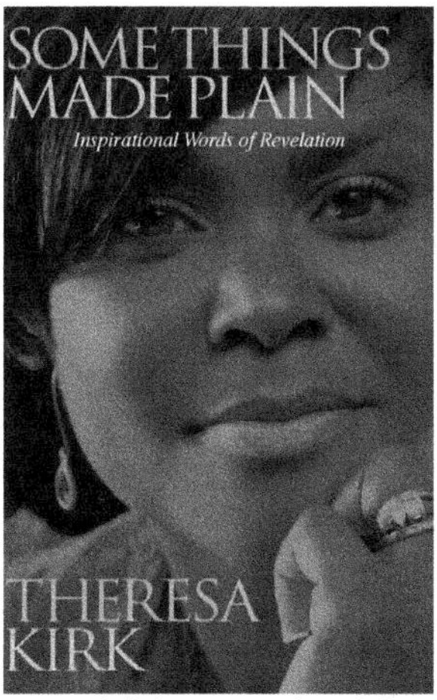

Some Things Made Plain - Volume 1

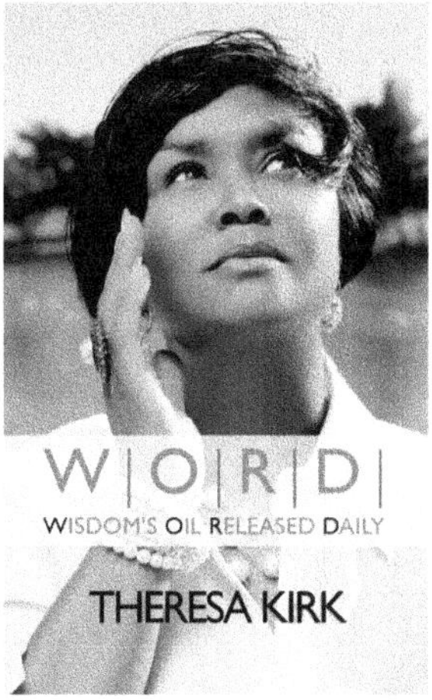

W.O.R.D. ~ Wisdom's Oil Released Daily - Volume 2

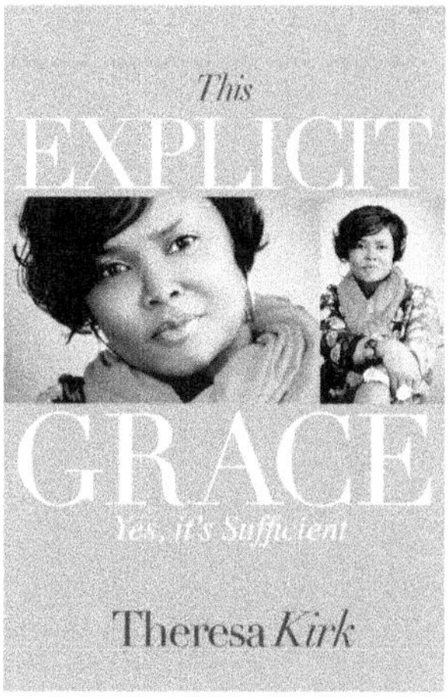

This Explicit Grace - Yes it's Sufficient - Volume 3

Coming Soon-Volume 4 ~ *It's That Simple*

Available at: www.knowledgepowerbooks.com
661-513-0308

www.ingramcontent.com/pod-product-compliance
Lightning Source LLC
LaVergne TN
LVHW021448080426
835509LV00018B/2202
* 9 7 8 0 9 8 5 4 1 0 7 7 3 *